Heroes, Villains
& Victims
·OF LEEDS·

Heroes, Villains & Victims

·OF LEEDS·

Stephen Wade

First published in Great Britain in 2007 by
The Breedon Books Publishing Company Limited
Breedon House, 3 The Parker Centre,
Derby, DE21 4SZ.

This edition published in Great Britain in 2012 by The Derby Books Publishing
Company Limited, 3 The Parker Centre, Derby, DE21 4SZ.

ISBN 978-1-78091-177-9

Printed and bound by Copytech (UK) Limited, Peterborough.

Contents

Preface		7
1	Temple Newsam Stories	9
2	Ralph Thoresby and his Society	13
3	John Green and Leeds Ware	16
4	Mary Bateman, Poisoner	20
5	John Nicholson, the Airedale Poet	25
6	The Engine Man: Matthew Murray	30
7	Resurrection Men	35
8	Edward Baines and *The Leeds Mercury*	39
9	The Man who Invented Concrete	46
10	Armley Gaol Tales	50
11	Chartist O'Connor on the Moor	57
12	The Dripping Riots, 1865	62
13	On Yer Bike in Victorian Leeds	66
14	The Arcades Story	75
15	Potts and his Clocks	79
16	Tetley's, A Leeds Icon	83
17	A Team of Victorian Businessmen	87
18	Berkeley Moynihan, Surgeon	92
19	The Coroner's Tales	97
20	A Dangerous Woman to Know: Louie Calvert	103
21	Gone for a Burton	110
22	'Don't Ask the Price, Everything's a Penny': Michael Marks	115
23	Some Leeds Victoria Cross Heroes	119
24	City Varieties People	123
25	Murder by the Parish Church	129
26	Brotherton and his Collection	134
27	Revie's Support Team	138
28	In the Cricket Hall of Fame: Len Hutton	144
29	Percy Scholes and the Love of Music	148
30	Poet Laureates? Austin and Harrison	152
31	Queen of the All Girls' Band	159
32	Villains Unknown, 1948	164
33	Short Stories 1: Strange People	170
34	Short Stories 2: Strong Characters	175
35	A Chapter of Accidents	184
Bibliography		190

Acknowledgements
For help in preparing this book, I would like to thank in particular
Laura Carter, who drew the line drawings, Liz Horsley, staff at West
Yorkshire Archives and library staff in Leeds and Hull and Leeds
United FC.

Preface

I was born in Leeds in 1948, and I've never had the Leeds taken out of me. I'm not sure what I mean by that, but I sense that it's a quality of acceptance, a certain dourness and a work ethic that won't lie down. As I write these stories of Leeds people through the centuries, I bring to mind men and women from my own family and they represent so much that is in these tales. My father's line, from Morley and Churwell, were farmers, miners and tanners. On my mother's side we had farmers, nurses, miners, clothiers and dressmakers. My parents and grandparents led working lives that represent a profound Loiner need to cling to the family and to values of friendship, openness and a sense of tradition. At least, they were around when I grew up in the city, going to Osmondthorpe Secondary Modern School in 1959 and leaving there in 1964 to work in the Saxone warehouse in Seacroft.

Leeds goes back a very long way in recorded history, being mentioned by the Venerable Bede in AD731 as 'Loidis'. It has been the centre of so many important historical events that there are too many to mention here, but anyone scanning the history of the city has to notice that we have always been involved in wool, engineering and clothing; Leeds folk have been fervent in their politics and their tussles over working conditions, and they have enjoyed a lively literary and artistic history. Queen Victoria opened the Town Hall in 1858, and there has been a *Yorkshire Evening Post* since 1890. In the Battle of the Somme virtually every street in Leeds lost some of its young men; the city suffered extreme air raids in World War Two and in 1959 the trams were taken away. I feel a part of that history because so much of it has come down to me from my family. I saw a milk delivery woman run over by a tram on Selby Road in the last year of their operation; I saw John Charles play at Elland Road and I was taught by the wonderful and learned scholar Stanley Ellis at the University of Leeds. Putting these words on paper now about my home city is particularly heartening and warm. We never forget our first locations.

Researching and writing these stories from history has taught me a massive amount of narrative, fact and sensation I did not know. I have been re-educated about the city of my birth. When I read about Leeds now, or walk her streets (she is female), I reflect on my arrival into this life, at the maternity home at Woodhouse, and I reflect that Woodhouse Moor, with its feast and students, was once a place where Feargus O'Connor drilled his troops in the Chartist years. That is just one of many stories I have to tell here; even if you know Leeds well, there will be something new for you.

My thanks go to Liz Horsley, Joyce Young, Andy Wade, library staff in Leeds and Hull, historians and scholars at the various places from whence I asked for help. I owe a great deal to the *doyen* of Leeds historians, David Thornton, and I owe a debt of gratitude to too many people to name here – all those who reminisced and let me listen.

This book is dedicated to my father, Albert Wade, who left Leeds to be a stoker in His Majesty's Navy and was then as passionate about Leeds United as I am now about dozens of lost causes.

ONE

Temple Newsam Stories

*'It's a mark of how little accepted Henry was as king
that to this day historians routinely refer to him as Lord Darnley.'*
(Alan Stewart, *The Cradle King*)

Visitors to the magnificent Elizabethan mansion Temple Newsam House tend to know two facts about it: that Lord Darnley (Henry Stuart) was born there in 1545, and that there is a ghostly presence in the house called 'The Blue Lady'. Leeds people usually know about that ghost and many of them have first-hand experience of the spirit, or at least know the stories. Lord Darnley has a poor reputation in film and literature, so the two facts are strange ones for a place with such a rich and eventful history.

The house was rebuilt by Sir Arthur Ingram in the early 17th century and again altered in 1796. It was bought by Leeds Corporation in 1922 and has been a popular site for concerts, fairs and all kinds of events ever since. It is only a few miles from the areas of Whitkirk, Garforth and Seacroft, and as a boy I used to walk there to have a summer picnic, past woods and fields, with ponds where my friends and I could fish for 'tiddlers'. But that personal memory says nothing about the history of the beautiful mansion seen for miles around.

Temple Newsam today is far more than a country house: it has a farm attached and an art gallery. Visitors from all over the world go there, and it is close to the A1 and M1 motorways, between Leeds and Selby, so it is hard to overlook its presence.

Darnley

Darnley's story is not a happy one. He married Mary, Queen of Scots, his first cousin, and their son was the future James VI of Scotland and James I of England. Mary and Henry married at the Holyrood Palace in Edinburgh, and it was a grand occasion but a hollow celebration for Henry, as he was only a pathetic token ruler with the title of 'King of Scots', which was only a reference to the fact that he was a consort and a figurehead.

Henry was only 19 when he married and it was a stormy affair. At the centre of his many hatreds and jealousies was the intriguing figure of David Rizzio, an Italian who was Mary's secretary. Such was the extreme destructive passion of the young husband that he arranged to have Rizzio killed, and he did it, with some helpers, in the presence of Mary. This was a certain formula for creating hatred towards himself and matters went from bad to worse for them. In 1567 there was a glimmer of hope for their future, but it did not take long for things to turn sour again and this time it was Henry who was the target for murder: his body was found in the gardens of Kirk o'Field. A man called Captain Blackature was arrested and hanged, but the business was far more complicated than that and he was surely a stooge. Historians tend to agree that Mary herself knew about the plot to kill Henry.

The main suspect was really the Earl of Bothwell, James Hepburn, and he abducted Mary later; it came as no surprise to many that the two were married not long after. Darnley was certainly a man with an anger-management problem, but he met his match when he went north of the border and began to 'play the king'.

It would be easy to say that Temple Newsam's tales are mostly sad and often tragic. The Irwin family, who owned the place for a long period, also found themselves in trouble at the time of the famous South Sea Bubble speculation in 1720, when many of the country's richest people were ruined. Luckily, they borrowed from the lord of the manor of Beeston, Alderman Milner.

Frances Shepherd

A quieter but interesting resident was Frances Shepherd, who married Charles Ingram in 1758. They really knew how to spend, and their grand home was to be embellished with items from the wealth that Frances brought with her, because she was from a rich Cambridgeshire family. Basically, she became mistress of the house and put into practice that kind of domestic economy and management that the 18th century so admired. The Age of Reason considered that the country house, and the deer park, lake, animals and hunting, was the epitome of the English aristocratic spirit; to manage such a place well was a huge achievement and a woman's reputation in that respect would go widely around the country.

What she did, in modern terms, was run a large business. It could be said that her task was made easier by the fact that she had good 'connections' and plenty of support in the network of family and friends around her, but the heart of her story is that she worked to overcome a bad reputation following her marriage, for that is what she came to Temple Newsam with. Basically, the people in her circle did not approve, and one of them, a powerful London lawyer called John Waple, wrote to tell her of his disapproval: 'I implore you with great truth that I have not met with one person that approves of it [your marriage] and if any of your female friends seem to do so, it is only to flatter your inclinations.'

Frances was made of stern qualities and knew her own mind. She also followed her heart, and she was happy. She even managed to cope with rather aggressive relationships and complaining attitudes in her servants.

The history of the site goes back a very long way: the Knights Templars were there (hence the name). In more recent times, there have been strong characters associated with the home, notably the Third Viscount Irwin, a supporter of William of Orange. He was a sporting type, with a lover of horse racing and cockfighting. When he was away fighting with Marlborough in the first years of the 18th century, he wrote home to do some recruiting, saying 'I know there are none better than the Yorkshire lads...I care not how many we have of them.'

The Blue Lady

However, the most notorious presence at Temple Newsam is surely the Blue Lady. There are several theories as to who she was (or is?). She has most often been seen in the Long Gallery and also on the great oak staircase. Over the years, visitors have often been shaken by the sight of her meeting their view as they turn into the Long Gallery. The most viable theory as to her identity is that she was Mary Ingram, the daughter of Sir Thomas Ingram, who died in 1652. The story is that she was coming home one day from Barrowby, not far from Garforth, when a band of robbers attacked the coach. Mary was dragged out and robbed of everything she had. Not surprisingly, it was a traumatic experience that affected her emotionally for the rest of her life. The result was that she lived in abject fear of being robbed, and that she developed the obsessive habit of hiding jewels in dark corners around the house.

Mary was supposedly a restless, troubled woman in life, and so she became a similar entity when she became a spirit haunting the house. People claim to have seen her moving fretfully about the place, no doubt desperately trying to find a new place to hide her jewels. We know what Mary was like, because a painting, probably painted by the famous Sir Peter Lely, is there for us to see. Poor Mary looks comfortable and self-contained, but then that is what a portrait was meant to do then, not showing the frantic fears inside her, deep down where she was so troubled that her spirit was destined to move forever around that magnificent building, harmless but often startling to visitors looking up from their guide books.

The residents have come and gone, but Temple Newsam goes on, a place of grandeur that will always impress visitors and leave strong visual impressions in the mind. Somehow it has a quality of unreality – so perfect, and yet from a time so far away from us in terms of our imaginations and how we can make the effort to reach back and visualise those lives of a class of nobility with time on their hands and projects to create.

TWO

Ralph Thoresby and his Society

'These gentle historians, on the contrary, dip their pens in nothing but the milk of human kindness.'
(Edmund Burke)

In my school 'House' in Leeds in 1960 there was a 'Thoresby House', but neither I nor my friends had any idea who Thoresby was. We should have been ashamed, because, as true Loiners, we ought to have known that Ralph Thoresby is the greatest of the Leeds historians. A Victorian reviewer noted that Leeds 'owed him a debt of gratitude', and that rests mainly on his historical works: *Ducatus Leodensis* (1715) and *Vicaria Leodensis* (1724). Yet anyone who does not know Leeds may surely ask why his work is so special and so important, as he wrote books which were, after all, merely local history.

Antiquarian

The answer can begin to be found in the fact that there has been a Thoresby Society in Leeds for a very long time, inspired by this man who was many things: a polymath in learning, a businessman, a diarist, a traveller and an antiquary. The last word is the key: in an age of gentlemen scholars he excelled in expressing an interest in all aspects of the past, and he started where common sense would direct any writer – to his own doorstep, Leeds. His family took an active part in the politics of the Civil War period, and they were Nonconformists. But later in his life Ralph abandoned the faith of his fathers and became a devout Church of England man.

At 19 he was sent to London and then to Holland, to learn and absorb gentlemanly virtues. It was an age in which travel was seen as an essential part of a young gentleman's education, normally involving a trip around Europe known as 'The Grand Tour', but, in Thoresby's case, fate was to step in and force him into a maturity well before the normal time; when Ralph was only 20, his father died. His mother had died when he was 10, and after his father's death he was left to take care of the business as well as his two younger siblings.

The business he inherited was in the cloth trade – the real heart of Leeds business – but he did not make much progress in that, and a little later in life he teamed up in Sheepscar with a businessman called Ibbetson and they worked in the production of rape oil. As an earlier writer points out, though, he was not suited to this 'But Thoresby, as in the course of his diary he himself declares, was not the man to make money in business; his choice of a partner was very unfortunate and when about 45 years old he withdrew from the business altogether.'

The Diarist

What Ralph Thoresby was really meant to do in life was follow learning and scholarly pursuits. He kept a diary and instinctively realised that the stuff of life around him every day was of value and interest: he understood that what men call 'history' is always being made. In the 20th century he would undoubtedly have been engaged in work related to documentary or oral history. But he also had wider interests: he monitored the social life around him, such as horse racing on Chapeltown Moor and the big freeze of 1684, when people were roasting oxen on the frozen River Aire.

Along with men like Samuel Pepys and James Boswell, Thoresby looked at life and found interest and curiosity in everything. He records a provincial society just before many of the first stages of the Industrial Revolution were to bring about massive change. Along with that writing and observation came recognition from the leading group of thinkers and men of letters of his day, the Royal Society. They elected him a Fellow in 1697. From his interest in the topography of the Leeds area and its past sprang a thirst for knowledge about everything that contributed to an historian's trade. In that part of a gentleman's life he began to be noticed early, writing the section on the West Riding for William Camden's magisterial *Britannia* in 1693.

There was one negative aspect to his success, however: so popular was he with his townsfolk that he was elected to the council of Leeds Corporation. He ought to have known that he would never find the time to fulfil those duties, and he clearly found himself involved against his better judgement. When he did manage to extricate himself, it cost him a fine, but he must have been glad to have more time with his books and maps.

Leeds Through and Through

Thoresby, a man born in the very heart of Leeds, in Kirkgate, died on 16 October 1725. He was 68, and a Victorian writer commented that Thoresby's hard work and money troubles shortened his life. But overall, a study of this extraordinary man's life provides a picture of a satisfied and fulfilled life; he married Anna Sykes of Ledsham in 1688 and appears to have found the perfect partner. His writing and reflections on his times provided a legacy of inspiration, a template for future Leeds scholars, and that is his achievement.

If we were to search for a dictum that might sum up his attitudes, it could be that 'Great events arise from little things.' That is something that explains the appeal of local history to many writers who now share Thoresby's passion for the particular, the local, the authentic in life experience. He knew all that, because he was not always confined to his study with his books – being as great and determined a traveller across land and sea as he was into the world of ideas and facts. It would make some sort of sense to think of him as the Dr Johnson of Leeds: a man who moved in a wide circle of friends, felt compelled to be endlessly curious and saw the link between books and life itself.

He represents not only a Leeds identity but also a Renaissance one; Thoresby had that enquiring mind which wants the cultural acquisitions of his time but also something else, a life with an intense vision about what knowledge is and what it is for. This deep enthusiasm was infectious and his circles of intellectual friends are the tangible proof of that quality in him.

THREE

John Green and Leeds Ware

*'For all I know of manufactories at the moment,
I had better be left alone...'*
(Josiah Wedgewood)

The year 1770 might be celebrated as the year of Wordsworth's birth, but it was also a momentous year in the industrial history of Leeds. It was in that year that the Leeds Pottery appeared in Jack Lane, a business enterprise in which Richard Humble of the colliery at Middleton linked with the Green brothers, John and Joshua. It did not take long for the phrase 'creamware' to be spoken in association with the name of Leeds. Ten years earlier the Leeds pot works was run by the Green brothers, but 'Humble, Green and Co.' was to be the firm whose name stuck.

The Designs

John Green was from Hunslet and he had the acumen and *nous* to see how things should be organised in the new outfit; the priority was to ensure that a waterwheel was built by the right people, so he engaged Hutchinson and Evers. That was followed by a

John Green.

change in the directors in 1783 and the publication of a book of designs. This was to advertise Hartley, Greens and Co. The title of the descriptive catalogue says everything that history has admired:

'Designs and sundry articles of Queen's or Cream-coloured Earthenware, manufactured by Hartley, Greens and Co., at Leeds Pottery, with a great variety of other articles; the same enamelled, Printed, or ornamented with Gold to any pattern; also with coats Of arms, Ciphers etc.'

The 44 plates were stunning; in all, this was an early example of exactly how to display to the world exactly what was on offer and just what craftsmanship lay behind the product's appearance.

Other catalogues followed, and there was even a forgery problem as Dresden capitalised on the product, but, as time went on, the strong man at the helm of the firm came to be John Green.

Extra Income

When there was a railway line constructed at Middleton from the collieries to Leeds, using the technical skill of Matthew Murray and Blenkinsop, it ran through the grounds of the pottery, so from this event in 1814 onwards the pottery received a rent for the use, along with a nice deal made to Green on the price of his coal. It was an early example of lateral solidarity in business: 'scratching each other's backs' in other words.

A truly significant development for Green came with the phenomenal success of the perforated creamware, known also as 'Queen's ware'. It was so successful and popular that for Victorians it became as well known as Wedgewood as a hallmark of excellence. Profits steadily climbed: in 1800 the yearly sales were around £30,000, a huge sum then, but profits were always steadily rising and the outlook was good by the mid-Victorian years.

The creamware was very distinctive, and in terms of how this was achieved (a deeper hue than a Wedgewood equivalent), the point is that the fine glaze was made by the application of arsenic. Hence we have an example of one of the typical side effects of Victorian enterprise – the cost in health to the workforce. The poor Leeds workmen suffered horribly from the arsenic, just as Cornish miners had done in their trade, and men were severely crippled after five years of work in the pottery. Changes were made, though, and by 1870 a commentator in a periodical noted that 'It is not now used.'

The Entrepreneur

Green, flushed with success, expanded and took the lead in establishing another pottery at Swinton. Green was a shrewd operator, being careful who he chose to look over partnership deeds and agreements, and letters survive showing his circumspection in that. But his good sense brought success: at Swinton the product was later known as Rockingham Ware, after a first name of 'Brown China'. One of the special products from here, collected widely since, is the Cadogan Pot. A description from the late Victorian period describes the peculiarity of this coffee pot:

> 'It has a small opening at the bottom to admit the coffee, but none at the top, and no lid. From the hole in the bottom a tube, slightly spiral, was made to pass up inside the vessel to within half an inch of the top, so that after filling, on the pot being turned over into its proper position for table use, the coffee was kept in without a chance of escape.'

We have to look far and wide for a better example of the ingenuity of designers of that period. It is a perfect example of the utilitarian frame of mind at the time – making objects of real usefulness but also attractive, and with an appeal that matched design with practicality.

Also produced, there was the famous dessert service made for William IV, now in Buckingham Palace. But perhaps most remembered in the annals of art and design from that period are the artists who worked for Green. He had men who each had a speciality in art work: there were series made with flowers, fruit, butterflies, landscapes and crests. In 1834 the Don Pottery was bought by Samuel Barker.

The Jug Made from a Killer's Bones

Of all the stories linked with Green's works, the tale of a jug made at Swinton is surely the most dramatic. The jug was made by Taylor Booth and shows flowers in groups, with jasmine depicted by the spout. The tale is that the main body of the jug was made from the fingers of Spence Broughton, who was put into a gibbet on Attercliffe Common in 1792.

Broughton has a street and a railway station named after him. Even as late as 1817 it was reported that his bones could still be seen in the wind. Apparently some potters were passing that way at night and they threw a stone at the skeleton, dislodging the finger bones. The jug was sold for £4 in London.

The growth of Green's firm was a success because of the right kinds of men, with special skills, being brought in as the business developed; obviously, the introduction of William Hartley as a designer in 1781 was a significant step towards major achievement. That distinctive look, with white Cornish clay showing richly through the translucent glaze, created the individuality, but on top of that it was the work of a succession of talented artists who maintained the quality and attraction. A visit to the Victoria and Albert Museum, for instance, gives the visitor a chance to see a teapot with a wonderful rich green patterning down the sides, bringing out the real appeal of the cream.

As with so many Leeds business success stories, there was a man at the centre who knew what his aims were, and a team around him who each had a particular talent. Creamware was there to stay, and now there are collectors across the world.

FOUR

Mary Bateman, Poisoner

'The coward's weapon, poison…'
(Phineas Fletcher)

York Castle has a long and often grim, disturbing history, and some of the most remarkable tales in the history of crime are set in this formidable and dark place. Not all of these stories have the glamour and myth of Dick Turpin, but they tell us a great deal about a turbulent period in English social history. One of the most evil residents of that dungeon was the Leeds poisoner, Mary Bateman, said by many to be a witch. She was born Mary Harker in 1768, and one writer about her says 'From an early age she developed great quickness which, instead of taking a direct course and developing into intelligence, was warped into low cunning.'

York Dungeon

The York prison cells housed many criminals, many poor unfortunate wretches, and some hardened killers during the years of English history, when the number of capital offences was in three figures and law and order were hard to find. But violence was rife at this time, with highwaymen and footpads everywhere, and riots always likely to break out among the underclass. One of the most heinous cases must be that of the young mother who murdered to make her way in life, and had even dabbled in black magic.

At five o'clock on a chilly Monday morning in March 1809, 41-year-old Mary Bateman was brought from her cell in York to keep her date with the hangman. Knowing that pregnant women were spared the noose, she had tried to 'plead her belly' to save her neck, but it was no use. A massive crowd gathered: they wanted their entertainment and to see justice done.

What had she done, this woman from Aisenby, near Thirsk, to come to such a sorrowful end? The jury were in no doubt that she had poisoned Rebecca Perigo of Bramley, Leeds. Her crime had been carried out in such a protracted and cunningly-planned way that her evil

Mary Bateman.

was deemed the more outrageous and callous. Mary had schemed to defraud Perigo, and she was clearly aiming to poison another victim who suspected her of the crime when she was apprehended. When arrested, a phial of deadly poison was found on her.

Crafty and Sly

Her offences were seen as even more devious and damnable when it was learned that she had attempted to practise witchcraft while she was in prison. She had extorted money from a young girl who wanted to see her sweetheart by sewing a charm and coins into her dress: a charm that would mysteriously force the young man she loved to come and visit her in the gaol.

Naturally, when it didn't work, the material was torn open and the coins were gone – in Mary's pocket. She had the knack of being able to put on a performance when required, and also to be as nimble and deceptive as the most skilled pickpocket.

Mary, while living in Leeds, did very well for herself by conning all kinds of people. One Victorian account of her crimes describes a typical ruse:

'The subject of this narrative contrived to ingratiate herself, as she well knew how, into the good graces of a family of the name of

Kitchin, Two maiden ladies of the Quaker persuasion who kept a small linen Shop near St Peter's Square in Leeds. There is every reason to suppose That she had deluded these unfortunate young women with some idea Of her skill in looking into futurity…For some time Mary was the Confidante of the Misses Kitchin…In the early part of September, 1803 One of the young women became very ill; Mary Bateman procured for her Medicines…These medicines were of a powerful efficacy and in the course of less than one week, Miss Kitchin died…'

Mary and her husband had first lived in High Court Lane when they came to Leeds, and from there she started her life of crime, beginning by stealing from a lodger and then working hard at obtaining property by deception. She even took money under false pretences from a poor widow and callously saw the children of her victim sent to the workhouse.

Trial and Retribution

At the trial, when Mary claimed she was pregnant, the scene almost devolved from solemnity into farce. The judge wanted a group of matrons in the court to examine Mary to prove her condition, and, as no one wanted to be involved, the good matrons of York began to shuffle out of the courtroom with some indignation. But the law prevailed. The judge ordered the doors to be shut so that the women had no choice but to comply, and Mary was duly inspected, pronounced not with child and the sentence passed. The trial had lasted for 11 hours. Mary had those harrowing words said to her as she stood there, the judge donning his black cap: 'The sentence of the law is, and the court doth allow it, that you be taken to a place whence you came, and from thence, on Monday next, to the place of execution, there to be hanged by the neck until you are dead, and that your body be given to the surgeons…May Almighty God have mercy on your soul…'

The gaoler, who was with her on her last night, noted that she wrote a letter to her husband and sent her wedding ring home to be given to her daughter. She had her youngest child in the cell with her, to suckle, and it was a scene that the ordinary (the officer who normally interviewed and monitored statements by prisoners) noted with feelings of sympathy. However, he also remarked on her silences regarding the crimes she had

PUNCH, OR THE LONDON CHARIVARI.—AUGUST 4, 1855.

THE USE OF ADULTERATION.

Little Girl. "IF YOU PLEASE, SIR, MOTHER SAYS, WILL YOU LET HER HAVE A QUARTER OF A POUND OF YOUR BEST TEA TO KILL THE RATS WITH, AND A OUNCE OF CHOCOLATE AS WOULD GET RID OF THE BLACK BEADLES?'

Punch picture on adulteration.

committed, and felt sure that she knew much more about other suspicious deaths connected with her activities. In the end, these secrets went to the grave with her.

At that time, noted killers and footpads attracted great crowds at their deaths, and Mary Bateman was no exception. Though there were no friends to swing on her legs and quicken her death, there was, nevertheless, a crowd to prove her status as a local celebrity. A massive crowd had travelled from Leeds, where she had murdered, to see justice done. The hanging took place at the new drop, behind the castle. It was eerily quiet when Mary said a prayer, but a shudder went through the crowd when she begged for mercy and shouted out that she was innocent.

Her body was taken away to be used for medical dissection – all the way to Leeds by hearse – but, as with all celebrity deaths, a general curiosity to view the body was provoked, and Mary's was a particularly successful crowd-puller. So many people came to look at her corpse that the money raised was £80 and 14s – a great deal of money then. It was given to the General Infirmary. This was due to the quick-wittedness of the enterprising William Hey, who saw a chance for some easy fundraising.

Mary Bateman was destined to be the subject of ballads, chapbooks and tales by the fireside for many years to come throughout Yorkshire, at a time when killers and robbers attracted more attention and sensation than conventional heroes. It appears that she was full of tricks and cons, even on one occasion having a hen appear to lay an egg with 'Christ is Coming' written on the shell. So she became the stuff of myth and tall tales. After all, this is the time when some children were told to be good or 'Old Boney' (Napoleon Bonaparte) would come and get them. Maybe others were threatened with a visit from the restless spirit of 'Mary the Poisoner'.

This Leeds killer is perhaps the best known of a host of similar criminals, people who saw an easy way to acquire some riches. As insurance developed, the temptations for this particular line of work grew apace, and in Liverpool the infamous case of the 'Black Widows', who killed several members of their own family, represents that temptation and its nasty, repulsive results. But Mary Bateman also had that other quality of the worst killer: stealth and subtlety, so that she won allegiance and trust before she struck with her deadly poison.

FIVE

John Nicholson, the Airedale Poet

'For all that generous Nature can bestow,
All Yorkshire scenes to Bingley-vale must bow.'
(Nicholson, 'On Bingley')

Poets are often related to places, and in the Romantic period of English poetry, that was often the case. In Yorkshire it was always common practice to refer to local poets as being especially rooted in a very specific neighbourhood, such as 'Bill 'o t' Hoyles' End'. But in John Nicholson, the writer always known as 'The Airedale Poet', we have someone who specialised in celebrating his immediate places, though he also wrote about Yorkshire more widely.

Nicholson's life was not, on the whole, a happy one. He was born in 1790 near Harewood, but his family moved then to Rombald's Moor. He was always a reader and had a literary cast of mind, coming to his adulthood at just the time that the great poets of his age were publishing and inspiring others. He had a teacher called Briggs, but we know little about this man, other than the fact that he played a significant part in encouraging the young poet. At Bingley Grammar School, managed by Dr Hartley, Nicholson excelled in English studies and began impressing masters with

John Nicholson.

his poetical ability. As is so often the case, it was at home that his interest in words and stories was developed, particularly from his father, Thomas, who often read aloud.

Early Success

The years around 1800 to 1820 were a period in which the middle classes took keen interest in 'untutored' writers, such as John Clare, the Northampton labourer, and, of course, Robert Burns. Nicholson may be compared to these in some way, as he left school early and was employed in wool sorting; yet, true to his type, he was far from being the ideal worker, often leaving the workplace behind and wandering on the moors. He would take a book and an oboe out with him; his musical ability led him into the literary and artistic circles, though, and there he met and courted Mary Driver, the 'muse' a young poet has to have, of course.

However, the first of many tragic events happened just a year into their marriage: Mary died during childbirth. He 'found religion' as a consolation and became devout Christian, being from a Methodist family. But the course of his life was never smooth, and he was a man of extremes. He may well have been a minister, but he married again: this time it was Martha Wild. Then, with some kind of domestic stability, he began to cultivate what might be called a 'literary circle', as was a common recreation then. It

John Nicholson's birthplace.

was an age of dinners, readings and debates in philosophical societies, and Nicholson gradually established a reputation, writing within a convivial community and seeing his poems go into local newspapers and periodicals.

At the centre of this success was his remarkable ability to write extempore. He tended to respond to any request on a special occasion. One evening, when with a friend at Carlinghow, Batley, he was told that a local man called Wilkinson, of Carlinghow Hall, had died, and he wrote these lines completely off the cuff:

'Dear Wilkinson is far above,
Drinking the draughts of heavenly love,
While I'm in a world of care
Listening to Hear My Prayer.
His prayer is heard. The harp of Heaven
Unto another bard is given.
My friend has joined the choir of heaven.'

It was always said that his reputation around Leeds and Bradford was made when he wrote a satire in 1818 – a humorous piece on a local doctor. But certainly his theatrical debut, *The Robber of the Alps*, made his name. He enjoyed the life around the two great cities, but, for unknown reasons, he moved to Harden and then Wilsden. With help from powerful friends, he finally made it into print with a local bestseller, *Airedale in Ancient Times*, in 1825.

Doomed to suffer

Looking at the portrait of him, reproduced in periodicals in the mid-19th century, we can see a rounded but handsome face, with a tinge of worry and concern. It is an image of a man who liked to be seen as a thinker, a man of good company and a ready wit. The warmth of his feelings shines out of that face. Here is a man who enjoyed good fellowship but could spend a long time brooding alone.

An early biographer wrote of this time in the poet's life, 'The intoxication of success gave a false colouring to everything that surrounded him: extravagant visions of fame and wealth floated before his mind's eye...' But in spite of this reservation, the work carried on at a level of good quality, his collection, *The Lyre of Ebor*, following hard on his first book.

Just as John Clare and William Wordsworth had eventually gone south and experienced London, so the Bingley poet went to the 'Smoke', and it seems that he was as whimsical and disorganised there as he was everywhere, only he was also careless about where he went and who with. The result was that he was detained and almost arrested by a magistrate (this was two years before there was a London police force). Martha had the necessary maturity and wisdom to keep an eye on him as a rule, but, left to his own devices, he often ran into trouble.

But there was one episode in his life that brought him out of that tendency to be dreamy and take an unrealistic view of life. This was following a commission from the factory reformer Richard Oastler. Oastler wanted Nicholson to write an epic poem with the theme of the factory children, and in fact the resulting poem was printed, paid for by the client. The reformer had stood before a committee of enquiry and spoken boldly of the terrible conditions of child labourers in factories, pointing out that the factory conditions in the Yorkshire towns would have 'disgraced a West Indian Plantation in the days of negro slavery'. Nicholson definitely saw the project through and also wrote a short poem called *The Little Piecener's Complaint*, and we have to assume that with dedication to that kind of social commentary in his writing he might have reached an even more exalted place in the writing fraternity of his time. But Nicholson was prone to indulge in drink too warmly and to put things off, maybe until the muse might visit him.

He was not one to write to order. While waiting, he drank too much and then, of course, he could not write to the standard he could achieve. As a Victorian writer said of him, 'After a short time the demon drink again asserted its crushing power over the helpless victim.'

Booze and decline

It is stunning to read today that when down and out in the grip of alcoholism, Nicholson had lots of support from dignitaries of the time, including the Earl of Harewood and Lord Ribblesdale. But despite his return to work, wool sorting at Titus Salt's mill, he was destined for a tragic end. Not only had the printer of his works been ruined and become insolvent, but the poet was also still trying to recover from the shock of the death of his child while he was in London. A combination of depression and drink made him vulnerable and weaker than previously, when he had often walked briskly in the open fields to clear his lungs and find subjects for verse.

One night – Good Friday 1843 – he was walking towards Eldwick and after trying to go across some stepping stones over the Aire at Dixon's Mill, he went into the water; he was found the next morning, dead of exposure. Maybe the best way to remember Nicholson is as a minor version, rooted in the Aire Valley, of Burns. His verses written when he looked at a freshly-drawn glass of porter typify this side of him:

'The gallant, the gay and the sporter,
Have here but little to stay,
For life's like the froth on that porter,
And quickly doth banish away.'

Leeds may never have had a writer of real literary stature in the years in which Wordsworth, Coleridge, Keats, Shelley and Byron flourished, but the city had a man who aspired to be that kind of poet. That he failed was down to many factors, but we can still admire his small-scale but enjoyable achievements. The titles of his publications give the reader a hint as to the kind of subjects and writing Nicholson enjoyed: such titles as *A Yorkshire Poet's Walk Through Knaresborough and its Vicinity* (1826) and *Low Moor Ironworks: a Poem* (1829). Maybe these were not immediately appealing titles, but the invitation to read poetry at that time was a particular experience relating to a class of readers with refined tastes. He was right for his time and for his peers. To find his work now, we have to pick around in antiquarian books, but perhaps that will change if some enterprising editor reads this.

Nicholson, in one sense, is the Leeds version of the stereotype of the 'poet damned'. The creative spirit suffering for art. His life mirrors, on a smaller scale, that of many more famous poets and artists, and perhaps, to a certain extent, he absorbed the myth and image of the poet in the sphere of sheer aesthetic exclusivity. That does not entirely hold water when we consider his writings on the contemporary world around him and on the social conditions in industry. But his life has that element of emotional turmoil we associate with poets like Coleridge at the time.

SIX

The Engine Man: Matthew Murray

'His trade was his only capital.'
(W.S. Cameron)

There are some figures in social and economic history who not only cause great changes themselves but influence others to a significant degree also. In terms of innovations and enterprise, few can equal Matthew Murray because, not only did he succeeded in his own special area of expertise, he collaborated with others to a high level and coped with a series of challenges both manfully and efficiently. For all these reasons he is a notable Leeds 'hero'.

He was not born in Leeds but came south from Stockton, where he was born in 1765. There were practical reasons for this, because he was looking for work to support his new wife and also escaping a local slump in employment. He was a man with a talent for inventing things – sheer expert problem-solving. In that special tradition of engineer-inventors he has won a place in the pantheon. The story is that he just walked south, down the Great North Road, with a pack on his back, looking for work. The myth of his journey to Leeds also includes the tall tale that he was penniless, and he arrived at the Bay Horse Inn and managed to persuade the landlord that he would soon have money to pay for his keep.

Matthew Murray.

Arrival in Leeds

But fortune was on Murray's side as well as skill and enterprise; he came to Leeds at a time when a cluster of other talented practical men and rare business minds were around the city. John Marshall, who has been inextricably linked with Murray's name as history has recorded their successes, was establishing himself in Adel, working in the production of flax. Murray took the challenge of producing a machine for use in flax production, which was to be very important in the growth of Leeds, and, after Marshall's move to Water Lane by the river, the flax industry in Leeds became the largest scale operation in the land, with 1,000 people working in the trade. One of Murray's flax machines was so successful that it won him his first distinctions – awards presented to him by the governments of Sweden and Russia.

Marshall was impressed by the young man from Teesside. A Victorian writer describes this:

> 'Something in the appearance of the young man – his frank face, and his intelligent, honest statement, doubtless, of what he could do – impressed Mr Marshall in his favour. He was engaged at once…Young Murray, turning his attention to the machinery, was able from the outset to suggest improvements that were carried out with such benefits to the employer that Mr Marshall, first having given him a present of £20, soon saw the policy of making him first mechanic in the workshop.'

Murray was clearly a great success there, but he was temperamentally made to be an individual with his own power-base and soon he was in business for himself. In 1795, teaming up with James Fenton and David Wood, he created the celebrated engineering works in Holbeck, which would be so successful that inventions began to emerge quickly and with a genuine impact; the first real innovation to be bruited around the industry was Murray's creation of a device that made use of the steam from the boilers to control and use the draught of the fire.

Industrial Espionage

Then came such things as a slide valve and an air pump. One invention, a planning machine, levelled off the surface of the valves in use. The outcome of all this was that he had refined and adapted so many components of production and engine functions that he was noticed by the massively-influential company of Boulton and Watt in Birmingham. The Birmingham engineering giants sent their man Murdock to Leeds to find out what was going on that such achievements were so radically successful. That visit introduced an element of Victorian hard business strategy to equal anything done by large-scale outfits in modern times, because Boulton and Watt, after the fact-finding mission, bought a piece of land next to Murray's company, to prevent expansion.

What was going on in that dark episode was no less than what is today called 'industrial espionage', but, apart from that, it was ungentlemanly and the work of what would then have been termed a 'blackguard' or a 'cad'. It is indicative of the way in which business in the years of the Industrial Revolution was headed.

Even worse was the return visit to the famous Soho Works in Birmingham: there was Murdock when Murray called in to do exactly what Murdock had done in Leeds, and a tour of the site was refused. Murray took this insult as a challenge, determining to take them on and carry on challenging them in any area of expertise that he could. He became undoubtedly the 'father of Leeds engineering' and concentrated energies on Holbeck, a place that became know in the locality as 'Steam Hall'.

Luddite Troubles

Like most of the West Riding businessmen, he suffered at the hands of the Luddites, the machine breakers. At the time many working men feared that the kinds of machines being made and refined by the Murrays of the world would certainly throw them out of work. The more aggressive side of this general discontent was the Luddite campaign, named after a mythical character called 'Ned Ludd' or sometimes 'King Ludd', who supposedly led the attackers when they came to the mills and factories that formed the threat to their lives. Mrs Murray becomes something of a hero too in this phase of the engineer's life. When the wrecking gang arrived, Murray was not at home, but his wife, apparently, from a window, told the assembled ruffians that she was quite able to defend herself and she fired a pistol at them. They ran off, and fortunately none of them were injured, or the consequences might have been dire.

The last years of the 18th century and the first decades of the 19th were also the years of the first experiments with producing locomotive engines. Richard Trevithick had been followed by the most important achievement in that respect, George Stephenson's *Rocket*; Murray was almost always a man who was a genius with modification, but in the case of railway construction and the achievement of making a locomotive for actual use rather than Trevithick's small-scale experiments on display circuits, he hit the jackpot with the Middleton Railway.

Here, he made the railway that carried coal from the Middleton Colliery in South Leeds, just beyond Beeston, to the canal. When Murray perfected his engine and took out a patent, he did so in the name of the colliery manager, Blenkinsop. The result has been that for generations of schoolboys, when they sat in the history class and learned about the Industrial Revolution and the 'age of inventions', they came across the phrase 'Blenkinsop's Engine' quite often, and the name may have stuck in young minds more than the name of Matthew Murray.

Middleton Railway

This engine had two double-acting cylinders and so a steady movement could be made without the use of a fly-wheel. It was run on a rack-rail, and a pinion wheel would integrate with this, so the engine and the rails were soon workable and the track fixed. The really important result of this was that gradients were not a problem. The tests and trials began in the yards and soon the time came for the opening of the Middleton Railway in June 1812. *The Leeds Mercury* reported:

> 'At four o'clock in the afternoon the machine ran from the coal-staith to the top of Hunslet Moor, where six, and afterwards eight, wagons of coals, each weighing three and a quarter tons, were hooked to the back part. With this immense weight, to which as it approached the town was super-added about fifty of the spectators mounted on the wagons, it set off on its journey to the coal-staith…'

The sight was indeed a prodigious one, attracting all kinds of visitors in the years following, as the fame of the engine and track spread. Even the future Tsar of Russia, Nicholas, came to see it. The great man from

Russia saw 30 loaded coal wagons moving at just over three miles an hour.

As Murray's interests were always wide, and he tended to move laterally in the engineering business, he was always busy on several projects at the same time; he even designed all the machine tools used in his own firm and many used by his peers in that world of invention and engineering – in all its contexts, as Leeds became famous for engineers and manufacture across a wide spectrum. So far did his interests extend, we can even point out that it was due to this that the gas supply to the city was streamlined and made more efficient. Naturally, many of these activities would spread to other places.

He died in 1836 and is buried in the cemetery at Holbeck by St Matthew's Church. Murrays were a presence in Leeds for some time, including one of his daughters, who married the Mayor of Leeds of 1844, Charles Maclean. But paradoxically for this man, whose achievements were so exceptionally important and whose products rivalled the greatest of his era, his reputation has been limited in the sense of his name being mediated and fixed in the public imagination. His name has never had that resonance that names such as Stephenson, Watt or Newcomen have had, in a wider national context. But as far as Leeds is concerned, he will always be a local hero.

SEVEN

Resurrection Men

'Body Snatcher: one who purloins bodies, newly buried,
to sell them to doctors for dissection.'
(*Brewer's Dictionary of Phrase and Fable*)

In Liverpool in the 1830s, gangs of people, in family groups, stood at the end of hospital wards where their loved ones lay dying, ready to fight off the resurrection men. They took such desperate measures because after the famous cases of Burke and Hare in Edinburgh, criminals of a nefarious turn of mind, saw bodysnatching as an easy way to earn money. Many northern towns were in the grip of cholera in the 1820s and 1830s, and York and Liverpool had particularly extreme problems in that respect. But the emergence of the 'resurrection men' was something that could happen in any part of the land.

Graves Robbed

There were so many cases of graves being robbed that an inventor with an eye to the main chance invented a coffin in which the corpse was fixed to the base, and the coffin itself was impenetrable by any normal type of hand tool.

This epidemic of grave robbing developed for a very simple reason: the schools of anatomy in the universities needed corpses so that their young medical students could practise their skills on 'the real thing' rather

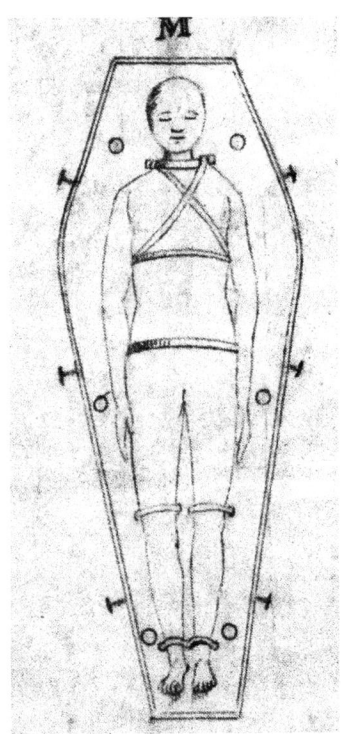

Design for a 'safe' coffin.

than by the study of drawings and models. But it was hard to come by corpses of good quality; if the bodies were being dug out of the ground, where they had been six feet under, all kinds of interferences had happened to them, not the least of which was the presence of maggots, of course.

The logical outcome of this was that doctors and professors really wanted newly-deceased bodies. From that came the moral problems, to say nothing of decorum, common respect and sensitivity. But Burke and Hare realised that it was easier to get a victim drunk, lead them into the dark, murder them and then take them to the anatomists' back door at night.

The Edinburgh Connection

Leeds, like most other places, had its resurrection men. One of the most well-recorded cases is of Thomas Daniel, who died in 1826 and was buried in St John's churchyard. But what happened was that the body of Daniel was found in Newcastle a few weeks later, when someone went to collect a box addressed to an Edinburgh resident. The man who collected the box and body was arrested and eventually sent to prison for six months. Then there was a similar occurrence when Tom Hudson hanged himself in 1831. But after burial he also surfaced later, this time at a pub, the Rose and Crown, as a body to be sold to the doctors. On that occasion a whole gang of snatchers were involved.

The whole nasty business became a fine art, as they often had to work quickly if they were bringing out newly-interred bodies. The trick was to leave the grave plot exactly as they had found it so that no suspicions would be aroused. Therefore, the neat way to operate was to dig down to the lid, prise off the lid smartly, deftly lift the body up and straight into a large sack. It was then an easy matter to put the soil back and replace anything else around the grave such as memorial stones, flowers or objects of remembrance.

But the temptation of the cash payments brought in others too – many who were definitely not experts at corpse removal. An instance of this was when children would be removed: something that may have seemed an easy task but was not, as in a case in Whitkirk in 1828 when the coffin was not even put back but simply left in a nearby lane.

Grave Clubs

Good citizens acted to try to stop this menace, of course. They often formed

Grave Clubs: these groups of very desperate and distraught folk would work out a shift system and have people posted on guard in cemeteries through the night, for the period in which the corpse would rot to such an extent that it would be worthless to any bodysnatcher.

Of course, some medical men would break the law in this horrible trade because they would encourage the snatchers to speed up the goods to meet demand. In Leeds a certain surgeon called Robert Baker was engaged in such criminal acts, spurred on by the thought that he could gain a good reputation as an anatomist. He paid a gang the handsome sum of four pounds – as much as they might earn in a month – to exhume a corpse. The difficulty for Baker came the next day when mourners went to the grave and found it empty. The snatchers had not cleared up after their dark deed. All a man could do in that dilemma was to try to pack the body off to Edinburgh, the centre of medical study and so a place that would regularly receive 'medical supplies'. Baker had to have the box and body left at an inn, where it would be collected on route to the north. But the smell gave the game away, the box was opened and the doctor traced and arrested.

Doctor and Snatcher

The trail led to the main snatcher, Armstrong. In court it was suggested that the doctor intended to sell on the body and make a profit – not to use it for medical purposes at all, but he denied that. As usual, it was the snatcher who got the rough end of things, and Armstrong was sent to prison in York for six months. Baker was acquitted; there was always the defence, perhaps slightly acceptable to some of the middle classes, that the study of anatomy had to go on and that Baker was engaged in necessary and essential research, but there always remained a dark shadow over any surgeon who was found out in this nefarious practice. His name would be linked to a stigma of reproach from that time onwards. Even some of the ruffians and desperate characters who became involved in the trade dared to state a similarly educational basis as their defence, as a man called Hodgson did in 1831, when he said in court:

'I was connected with a medical man in the taking of this body and it was for the purpose of mutually dissecting it. I could not give up his name without utterly ruining him, and if you send me to prison you will ruin my prospects for life…'

The plea had some kind of beneficial effect because his sentence was only six weeks in York. The body Hodgson had provided for the medical men must have given them an extra challenge as they worked: the man who died had fallen into a dye-pan full of hot liqueur – no doubt forensic evidence on the limbs of the snatcher was not difficult to notice and use against him.

The cases recorded and described in reasonable details in the papers of the time make it clear that the circuit of the trade was well established: corpses exhumed in Leeds, taken with haste and in darkness to an inn that was a posting-house, would be placed close to the Great North Road and from there collected and taken to Edinburgh. The essential elements in that process were secrecy and speed.

The Anatomy Act

What changed all this was the 1832 Anatomy Act, which made it easier for doctors to access corpses, as it was legal to dissect bodies after that. The key words in the law were that a surgeon could arrange matters with patients so that they could direct and give permission: 'Any person could direct that his body after death be examined anatomically.' It was a sensible move that should have been done many years before, and, in fact, as soon as the Burke and Hare case became public knowledge. The impact of those two Edinburgh killers was profound: the word 'Burker' as a term for the 'profession' stuck and was part of the English language and in regular use for many decades after the man's end on the scaffold.

In Leeds conditions were just right for this trade: it was a city growing greatly day by day, it had a population concentrated in a confined area with a very large number of beer houses and inns, and it had a medical fraternity with drive and ambition to succeed. Often they grew tired of waiting for the bodies of hanged felons and were well aware that their students were eager for real professional training.

An anatomy lesson.

EIGHT

Edward Baines and The Leeds Mercury

'We live under a government of men and morning newspapers.'
(Wendell Philips)

Philips, writer of the above quote, could have applied his comment well to Edward Baines, a man whose main achievement may be summed up neatly with the point that he bought a Leeds newspaper which was beginning to struggle to get by and made it a huge success. Yorkshire stalwarts will have to forgive Baines for being a Lancashire man in his origins, but his life and work clearly put his nature in the white rose county.

Early Years

Edward was born in Preston in 1774, the son of an excise officer, and he went into the textile trade. He was employed by Thomas Walker, a printer, and learned the rudiments of the business there, but soon he was on the move and came to Leeds.

In the late 18th century, when Baines's story begins, newspapers were an absolute necessity of life, and English people were partly defined by their habit of reading and talking endlessly

Edward Baines.

about what was in the news. The age of the coffee house, as a centre for debate, discussion and often meetings of clubs and societies, was also the age of the newspaper. Periodicals had also boomed since the first few years of the century, with the *Spectator* and the *Tatler. The Times* had been around since 1758.

In the regions, printers had also multiplied in the 18th century and local newspapers were an essential part of everyday life. Naturally, they were aligned with political parties, or at least with political positions. In Leeds, when young Baines arrived looking to use his knowledge of printing to build a life for himself, the country was currently torn apart intellectually by the events in France. The French Revolution had had a massive effect on life in Britain, with the fear of sedition and even revolution in the streets very much in the air. In 1799–1800 the Combination Acts were passed, preventing people from gathering in small groups in the streets to talk and express ideas. Publications of all kinds could easily fall foul of the law by being termed 'seditious' for opinions expressed in their pages. Leeds was thought of at the time as the 'hotbed of sedition' by many, and some of the trades in the town were notorious for nurturing dissenting views of politics.

The *Mercury*

Into this situation came Baines, seeing that one newspaper, *The Leeds Intelligencer,* had become the organ of Tory views. The other paper, the *Mercury*, was really nothing substantial and had no clear idea of its identity and production values. In 1801, with help from Whig supporters, he took over the *Mercury* and energised it. The move involved a massive loan of £950 – and that was after an initial loan from his father (£1,000) to set himself up as a printer in Leeds. *The Leeds Mercury* had been established in 1718 by John Hirst. It was originally a 12-page affair in quarto size, totalling around 5,000 words. All papers that were just a single sheet were due for stamp duty, so it cost only three halfpence. The basic concept for this paper was that it summarised London news and gave a very short mention of local events and issues. By 1739 the paper was folio size, then being owned and produced by James Lister.

Griffith Wright's *Intelligencer* came along and the *Mercury* died for a while, revived in 1767 by James Bowling. Finally, in 1794, he sold it to the firm of Binns and Brown, and with them it languished. But then along came Baines. His son, writing his father's biography, expressed the impact of Baines thus:

'That the reader may form an idea of the improvement effected in newspapers during the period that the Leeds *Mercury* was in the possession of Mr Baines, the following comparison is given on a single point, that of dimensions:

Number of words in a copy of the Leeds *Mercury* in 1801 – 21,376

Ditto.....................in 1848, 180,000 words.'

Obviously, the existing papers, with their political leanings, would have major features on news regarding events that could be presented with the bias expected by the readers. But as to other material, such as law reports, documentary correspondence, features on local personalities and so on, they were not really interested.

As Baines went on and the years passed, he was often embroiled in the issues of the day. The effects of the end of the Napoleonic War in 1815 led to one major involvement on the part of Baines and his paper: the crisis emerged partly due to the Corn Laws, as these strict measures kept the price of corn high and so the working classes suffered grievously. This added to an existing restlessness and dissatisfaction and, of course, the army veterans and crippled were returning home in their thousands. There was extreme poverty in many areas; in desperation, the government began to use informers and *agents provocateurs,* planting spies among the workers, as it was to do throughout the coming problems with Chartists and Luddites.

The Spy Network

Baines caused a sensation when he released the news that there was a spy around Leeds in 1817: a man called William Oliver had indeed been busy as an *agent provocateur.* Of course, these types were despised. They worked subtly among the workers and dissenters, putting on an act of friendship, buying drinks in the inns and all the time listening to conversations and noting any plans made. They also pointed out the most dangerous leaders among the more aggressive rebels or malcontents. Oliver had worked in Dewsbury and there he had forced those with a mind to bring about a violent revolt to act, monitoring affairs for his masters of course. What Baines did was obtain the facts of Oliver's activities and then tell the whole story, the turning point being the arrest of 10 men by General Byng at Thornhill-Lees. Baines wrote of the despicable Oliver and the resulting arrests:

'From everything we have heard of the character and conduct of General Byng, we are persuaded that he has been merely the medium for receiving Oliver's information; and that whoever may have employed this double-distilled traitor, the general has acted merely in discharge of his duty. But every circumstance we have just related proves that somebody has employed him and the question is – who were his employers?'

It had an effect: Lord Liverpool, the Prime Minister, came clean about the use of Oliver and his like, and for Baines it was a huge public relations coup. The words from the *Mercury* were read aloud in the House of Lords by Earl Grey. The story emerged that spies had been used to encourage insurrection.

Baines expressed the nature of the work done by Oliver and his kind in this way: 'The materials at most were existing, which he so assiduously gathered together and worked up into a conspiracy…' Of course, around this same time – in 1819 – the most infamous and revolting move made by that repressive and paranoid government happened in Manchester, with the Peterloo Massacre. There, what began as a meeting of workpeople in regular order to listen to the famous speaker, Orator Hunt, ended in a charge of hussars and the slaughter of many ordinary Manchester folk.

In 1834 Baines became MP for Leeds after Macaulay had resigned his seat. Baines was chosen as the Liberal candidate, replacing Sir John Beckett narrowly; he supported such measures as abolishing church rates and a bill to let marriages of Dissenters be registered. One of his passionate engagements with issues of the time was the subject of factory legislation and child labour, though his views were not entirely those of reformers such as Oastler.

Mechanics' Institute

Baines also played a part in the growth and success of the Mechanics' Institutes. It was between 1824 and 1826 that these organisations began.

The artisans of the Industrial Revolution were clamouring for a wider education and also for a chance to play a part in the rise of self-education. They had been a part of the scene since 1800 and there was talk of Leeds joining in that movement for quite some time; then, after Dr Birkbeck had created the London Mechanics' Institute, a precedent had been set. Baines backed the campaign energetically. After a major article was printed in the paper in 1824 a meeting was held to consider the next step. Some local celebrities were there, including Benjamin Gott and Dr Hunter. After a meeting in April a prospectus was issued. The institutes began with a library and the formation of a reading room, and the Leeds pioneers planned it carefully.

The rationale was put this way:

'...a very large portion of the working classes and apprentices of the town, who could not or would not follow scientific pursuits, might thus derive benefit from the institution, and the number of subscribers would in all probability be increased.'

They were right. The sense of triumph and celebration is evident in an address printed in the paper in December 1824, and in 1825 the institute was opened in Park Row.

When it came to the exciting period of 1831–32 as the move towards the Great Reform Act created debate and agitation everywhere, writers, editors and commentators on current affairs were writing about who might or might not get the vote. The focus for many was on the proposition that £10 freeholders would get the vote. Baines, again, was in the thick of things and once more he set to work to actually achieve something definite. He did a Leeds survey to find out how many and who these potential freeholders might be in the

HISTORY,

DIRECTORY & GAZETTEER,

OF THE

County of York;

WITH

SELECT LISTS OF THE MERCHANTS & TRADERS OF

London,

AND THE PRINCIPAL COMMERCIAL AND MANUFACTURING

Towns of England;

AND A

VARIETY OF OTHER COMMERCIAL INFORMATION:

ALSO A COPIOUS LIST OF THE

Seats of the Nobility and Gentry of Yorkshire.

BY EDWARD BAINES.

THE DIRECTORY DEPARTMENT BY W. PARSON.

IN TWO VOLUMES.

VOL. I.—WEST RIDING.

ILLUSTRATED BY MAPS, PLANS, &c.

Printed and Published

BY EDWARD BAINES, AT THE LEEDS MERCURY OFFICE;

AND SOLD BY

HURST AND ROBINSON, 90, CHEAPSIDE, LONDON,

AND ALL OTHER BOOKSELLERS.

1822.

The title page from Edward Baines's book.

town. Lord John Russell in London had the results, and the data provided hot material for debate. The canvassers in Leeds had found that 'In the parts occupied chiefly by the working classes, not one householder in fifty would have a vote…Out of 140 householders, heads of families, working in the mills of Messrs Marshall and Co., there are only two who would have votes…'

The Man and his Nature

Baines was a meticulous and dedicated professional. He also appears to have had time for everyone in his business. One story told of his watching a young apprentice fold a sheet of newspaper. The boy folded it several times, and there was a wrinkle across the first sheet at the first fold. Baines watched him and then said, 'Jim, it is a bad thing to begin wrong.' As his son commented, 'The poor fellow had found it so, for he soon fell a victim to his vices and every succeeding fold of his life was easy and straight. The lesson is worth remembering.'

Edward Baines became seriously ill in his 76th year and his wife, looking after him when the end was close, was aware that it was the 50th anniversary of their marriage. His son wrote a touching and sensitive account of the last days, noting that some lines from Isaac Watts were read to him:

'A guilty, weak and helpless worm,
On thy kind arms I fall;
Be thou my strength and righteousness,
My Jesus and my all.'

To which Baines responded, 'Most beautiful'. He died shortly after that, on 3 August 1848 – the year of revolutions in Europe, something that would be filling pages in the beloved *Mercury*. As his son wrote, 'In Leeds there was a very great mourning. With an honourable oblivion of party distinctions, the inhabitants lamented him a good man, a public benefactor, and vast numbers almost a father.' He is without doubt one of the heroes of the history of Leeds, playing a major role in the identity of the city as it expanded in the years of Victorian prosperity.

When the Bradford journalist James Burnley wrote a sweeping study of Victorian businessmen late in the 19th century, he was writing at a time when the doctrine of Self Help, as advocated by Samuel Smiles, had indeed had a massive impact on the men and ideas of the century. Baines does fit the pattern of the 'self-made man', but of course he was reaching his successful years well before Victoria's reign began in 1837. For that reason he surely shows some 'Regency' virtues, mainly that he was producing news and features at the moment when revolution was in the air and Britain was preoccupied with the question of how to defeat Napoleon. His life relates more to the pattern of the man of principles mixed with the artisan: he learned a trade and from those skills came a sure political commitment and a series of social crusades.

History will perhaps judge and assess Baines as a man to put alongside some of the newspapermen who have always formed opinions and made them have an impact – men like Russell of *The Times* for instance.

NINE

The Man who Invented Concrete

*'We know relatively little of how Victorian cities
were actually built except that in the early and middle years building
was left to speculators of limited resources...'*
(Asa Briggs)

Most Leeds folk probably walk past the small blue plaque in Albion Place – but there it is, telling us that Joseph Aspdin invented cement. There is no doubt that his name ought to be better known – he's a real unsung hero, almost the definition of that cliché.

Aspdin called his substance 'Portland' because the colour of the concrete he made reminded him of the colour of the famous Portland stone quarried down in Cornwall. What he did was make something that was easy to mix and would harden when in contact with water, of course. At the time, the making of cement was tough on the workers involved and there was resistance to it, but despite the thinking of Aspdin's contemporaries, that it would only really have a use in the construction of bridges and dams, it was a massive success story. Aspdin must have had no idea just how profound

Memorial blue plaque for Aspdin, Albion Place.

the impact of his material and production were going to be in Victorian England and far beyond. Of thousands of patents for a variety of new devices in that age of invention, this was one that was destined to be really revolutionary.

The Discovery/Rediscovery

The Romans knew about building: it was one of the main reasons why they made a vast empire. The Egyptians used heat-fired lime, gypsum and water to build with, and that mortar from those ingredients made the pyramids. Clay was used by the Romans in their version. A fine example around today of the Roman achievement is the castle of San Angelo, built in Rome around AD138; although the stone facing has been stripped away, the exposed concrete is still solid and in fine condition.

What Aspdin did was rediscover these things: he ground together limestone and clay, and so the resulting substance, after pulverising, would be a different chemical composition. The substance was then formed into a mass like a bundle of mixed powdered stone aggregate and the final powder mixed with gypsum. All that was needed then for the wonderful item we call concrete was water. It was a momentous achievement. Aspdin knew it, because he built a high wall around his work yard and was sensitively aware of being 'ripped off', should anyone in the trade know what he had achieved. There was Portland cement and the buyers were waiting.

He had produced all this in his kitchen. What he had made was hydraulic cement. Just four years later, the tunnel under the River Thames was made with the use of Portland cement. By 1871 it was used on a huge project – produced in Pennsylvania. That wall around the workshop could only work for so long: the wide world needed the materials, and fast. It was a time when patents were not entirely preserved and defined, so trouble was to come along with the triumphs.

Crucial at the Great Exhibition

In 1846 a writer representing the company that sprang from Aspdin's work, Maudes, Jones and Aspdin, was well aware of poor copies and inferior versions of their cement and it was a problem. He wrote:

'Sir, In the spring of last year we supplied a large quantity of

Portland cement for the Royal Exchange Building in Cornhill. And within the last few months an article also called Portland cement but not supplied by us has been used at number 82, Cornhill, and has signally failed. Owing to the similarity in the name, a very general impression exists that the cement which has failed was of our manufacture....'

Aspdin's firm was rightly outraged; what was the use of a patent if you suffered that kind of work by a crook? Their name was being sullied. Their letter to the paper was a forthright attempt to clarify for the public the fact that they were still about quality: their name was maintained by reputation. It was becoming a general problem, though, because they were aware that 'Many other failures' had occurred in 'other parts of the country'. By that time, the company was really placed at the heart of industry – in Rotherhithe, by all major communication and transport routes.

They were exonerated and reassured, one hopes, in the Great Exhibition of 1851. At that huge and chest-beating display of British and Imperial art, craft and industry, they were there, in the very integuments of the materials and objects being shown to the world. For instance, the firm of Bazley, White and Co. had produced a beam of hollow bricks, and that went to a trial of strength before the public. *The Times* wrote that 'The brick beam was identical in size with that of common bricks and Roman cement constructed at Nine Elms in 1833. But at the Exhibition, the Bazley bricks were held together with Portland cement and had thin bands of iron running through them. A first mighty load of pig-iron failed to affect the beam. Then it took a huge load of 62,800 pounds weight to even cause a slight crack. Then the abutments were thrown out of the perpendicular.'

'The Prophet Samuel in Infancy'

In Leeds there is one other Aspdin survival. In the School of Civil Engineering at the University of Leeds there stands a statue made by Joseph's son, James. This is *The prophet Samuel in Infancy*, now known as *Little Sam*. It was realised that a copy would have to be made, as the original was, of course, subject to easy damage. Lecturer John Baily set about the task, using latex and latex thickener to make the mould required, and it was a success. There was then a mortar version made, with great ingenuity and care. The resulting *Sam the Second* is now apparently at the University of Dundee.

It seems entirely fitting that technology and sheer concern for preservation in the home town of the inventor should help disseminate the Aspdin name. In time, more heads might turn and notice that blue plaque, a minor detail of colour in the midst of all the hurrying shoppers. But, nevertheless, a true Leeds hero.

TEN

Armley Gaol Tales

'After defying police and firemen for hours at Leeds yesterday...
A man who escaped from Armley Gaol was finally overpowered when a
police Sergeant threw pepper in his face and hurled his truncheon at him.'
(*The Times*, 1945)

The magnificent but forbidding sight of the castellated features of Armley Gaol still stand towering over one of the valleys of Leeds, and the reputation of the place is still one of a harsh regime. The cells have seen many of the most notorious villains in history, as have the places that used to be the death suite and scaffold. It opened in 1847 on the penitentiary model, radial wings from a central tower. At first, as the plans for the design show, there were to be separate areas for women and children, including cells and exercise yards. It is surely a place where, if one believes in such things, ghosts could wander the wings. In that

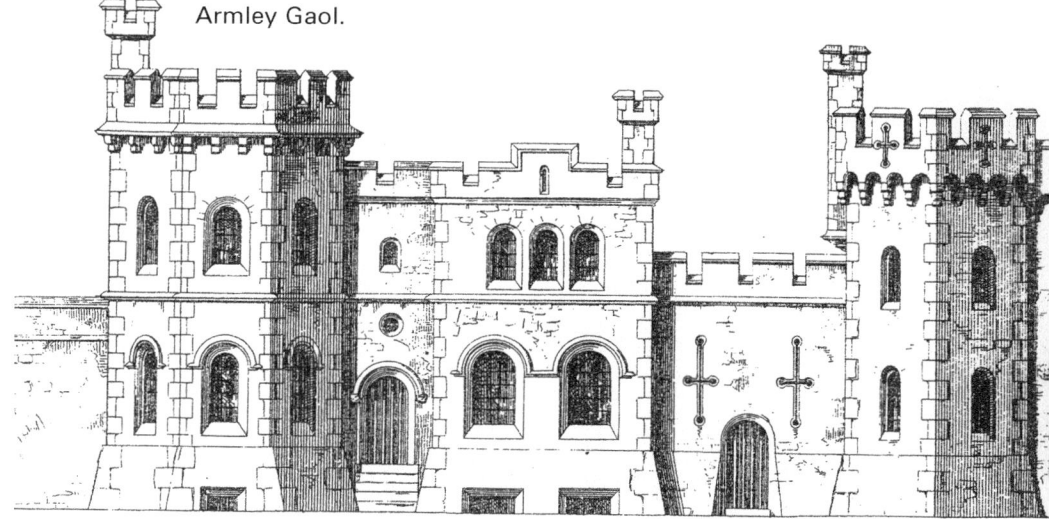

Armley Gaol.

massive place there have been murderers, robbers, bombers, psychopaths, gangland leaders, criminally-insane types, women under mental duress who have killed their babies, and even the less violent but more deviously-cunning plotters and forgers of the underworld.

Scaffold Stories

In the 19th century one of the main deterrents for murderers was surely the fact that, should they ever end up on a scaffold, the hangmen would not give them a quick death. Many of the early hangmen were people with drink problems. One of these was Thomas Askern of York. Typical of his actions was the execution of the Sheffield killers Myers and Sargisson. So desperate was Myers to avoid the noose that he tried slitting his own throat, but the regime had to follow the dictates of the law, and if a man was to hang, then hang he would. Myers was stitched up and taken to hang. The two men were despatched in the only public execution outside the prison (public executions ended in 1868); typical of the humanitarian limitations of hanging then, Myers died quickly but Sargisson took several minutes as he struggled on the end of the rope. Grotesquely, the slit throat of Myers bled profusely and the corpse was soaked in blood.

The most notorious killer of the age of hanging to be sent to his death at Armley was surely Charles Peace. Peace was, in the 1870s, the kind of criminal whose adventures reached popular culture and mythology. He

James Berry – executioner.

was hanged by a man who was more expert in his craft: William Marwood from Horncastle, who had perfected the 'long drop' method and thought that a villain should die by asphyxiation, not strangling. Peace had killed two people, one a man whose wife Peace was harassing, a Mr Dyson, and the other a police officer, Constable Cock, at Whalley Grange. The officer advanced on Peace with his truncheon, ignoring a warning shot fired over him, and when he kept coming Peace fired the revolver.

Most thrilling of all the Charlie Peace stories was his attempted escape from a train. He had been arrested in London while living and operating as a criminal under a false name; as he was being escorted back to Leeds for trial, he persuaded one of his guards to let him relax his vigilance for a minute and Peace leapt from the train. He was severely injured and soon retrieved. He must have known the game was up when he was identified in Newgate prison by a policeman from Yorkshire who confirmed the crook's real identity.

On the scaffold at Armley in February 1879 he said he was being killed 'For that I done but never intended', and when Marwood put the white hood on Peace's head he said his final words: 'My last thoughts are for children and their mother, a wonderful woman, they mustn't worry about me. I know where I'm going. I am going to heaven.' It became a Victorian narrative image of renown, so much so that Madame Tussaud created a tableaux from the scene. In 1929 there was a show at the Ambassador's Theatre in London called *The Misdoings of Charlie Peace*. Such was the fascination with the man that this purported to be 'a report in 16 instalments of the life of Charlie Peace between August 1 1876 when he was working as a framer and gilder...to the condemned cell in Armley Gaol...'

There were plenty more Armley hangings, but perhaps few so emotionally complex and harrowing as the double execution of a couple who had murdered the woman's husband. Wife and lover died together, but it was the hanging of the woman that affected the hangman John Ellis very deeply. On the day they were hanged, Emily Swann had said to her lover 'Good morning John', and he, the man who had beaten her husband to death, returning to the marital home to finish off the man he had already assaulted, said quietly 'Good morning love.' Ellis, in his memoirs, wrote 'She was 42 years old, a little stumpy, round-faced woman, only 4 feet 10 inches tall and 122 pounds in weight. She was the first condemned woman I had ever seen, and frankly I didn't think the authorities would allow her to go to the scaffold.' But they did.

Ellis, when he heard the last conversation between the two condemned, reflected 'This, I had to confess, was an astonishing scene, a dialogue between two people, one of them a woman, standing with pinioned arms and legs, faces blotted out by shapeless white bags and with ropes fixed around their necks.'

The very last person to be hanged at Armley was Zsiga Pankotia in June 1961. He killed Eli Myers in Chalwood Avenue, off Street Lane in Leeds, his victim being a man who had foolishly bragged about the money he had won on the football pools. Pankotia broke into Myers's home with the intention of merely stealing something, but Myers disturbed him and Pankotia took hold of a bread knife. A desperate struggle then began as Myers took on the intruder; Myers was stabbed to death and Pankotia drove away in his van.

It was to be a complex case, because Myers had a heart condition, confirmed by the famous Dr Poulson of Leeds University. The issue was: was Myers the market trader killed or did his weak heart fail in the fight? The jury had no problem finding Pankotia guilty, and he was the last client of Mr Harry Allen, hangman, at Armley.

Escapades

In 1958 two 'rather dangerous characters' escaped from Armley in the night. Michael Millard and Royal Pettinger managed to force the bars on their cell window, but a third man was captured in the grounds. Somehow they went out of the grounds, presumably over the wall. But there were more desperate conflicts between prison inmates and staff. In 1962 a prison officer was attacked, being found on open ground in Huddersfield. He was an officer in Armley, and he had been beaten up after a car stopped and pulled him inside. Someone had a grudge, it seems.

Van Dieman's Land – destination of many felons.

The thrill of the chase in trying to recapture escaped villains happened on a grand scale in 1945 when a man escaped on VE day, hid in houses and was on the loose for 15 hours. Albert Dalby had been sentenced to two years for a number of offences, including shopbreaking. He managed to take a car, and he was shadowed by police from Leeds to Pontefract and then on return to Leeds. After a smash involving two cars he ran off, and it was noted that he had a gun in each hand.

Finally, in Camp Road, he was cornered by large numbers of police and detectives. The first ploy was to call in the fire brigade and to fire a jet of water into the house. Dalby staggered onto the roof and then went back in again as water was fired at him. By mid-afternoon the army arrived and tear gas was used. As officers closed in, he was on the attic stairs and as three men from the CID approached him, with a sergeant, the sergeant threw pepper into Dalby's face and then hurled his truncheon at him.

The hero of the day was Sergeant Robinson. As for Dalby, he was charged with the attempted murder of two police officers.

One notable failure, with a strong element of farce, was when a prisoner had a roast chicken given to him by his wife, which inside contained hacksaw blades. An officer caught the man using the blades to saw through the bars. Other people were implicated, but the main result was that the man was given another 21 months in gaol. Escape attempts have been very common, but few as rash and foolhardy as that one. The officer may even have been amused, we might guess, when he saw the man at work, no doubt fairly noisily.

Changes

Basically, the gaol was indeed designed as a fortress. The oldest part has the radial four wings, and it covers around eight hectares. When it first opened it could boast 334 cells. Today, as part of the modern prison service, an adequate description of the gaol would have to include such things as a gymnasium, healthcare, help with drug problems, a chaplaincy and all kinds of support for prisoners and their families. We have to reflect that the Victorian prisoners, with their long hours of physical labour and thin gruel, would not recognise the place.

The main idea behind a Victorian prison was that it should remake the offender by means of the 'dignity of work' and ample time for remorse and repentance. The Armley men would have had the opportunity to put up with the labours of prison routine, such as making sacks, gardening, working with oakum, tailoring or cooking. For some, this would have worked, but we have very little in our minds today about that side of gaol. The men were, as one said, 'alone with God and a wounded conscience', and that does not make for dramatic narrative. What has come down to us more forcibly is the image typified by that of Charlie Peace, put into Madame Tussaud's Chamber of Horrors with the hope that his wax effigy might lead people to have moral reflections on the nature of evil.

ELEVEN

Chartist O'Connor on the Moor

'For Chartism was in these manufacturing areas a cry of distress, the
shout of Men, women and children drowning in deep waters...'
(Mark Hovell)

Woodhouse Moor, the place just beyond the University of Leeds, is usually accustomed to being a place when Leeds people would see and visit the feast: a typical weekend place where children can have fun. Centuries ago it was the common land where people could graze their animals. In 1870 it was one of only two large green areas for recreation, along with Bramley, but the late Victorian period was a time when parks and gardens burgeoned so that the workers could enjoy walks, brass band music and sport. All this is very leisurely and calm. But in the 1830s it was the scene of activity by the 'Physical Force' Chartists, led by Feargus O'Connor. He saw it as an ideal place to 'drill the troops' of the more aggressive Chartists who thought that working men would not get the vote: they would have to take it.

O'Connor was an Irish barrister, born in 1794. His deep radicalism made him espouse the Chartist cause in England, and he became MP for Nottingham in 1847. He was a powerful public speaker and his charisma helped the movement for political reform to gather momentum in the 1830s and 1840s. Mark Lovell sums him up with these words, a mixture of racial stereotypes and a judgement on his source of power, 'O'Connor was a big, rather handsome looking man endowed with great physical strength and animal feelings...As an

Irishman he dearly loved a "row" and was supremely in his element in such Donnybrook affairs as the Nottingham election riot of 1842.'

Chartism

Chartism was the movement for pressing the reform of the franchise in England, spanning the years 1837 to 1854. At the heart of this radical line of thought was the desire to make a parliamentary party that represented the working man. Those working people mostly thought of the movement as a question of basic needs, not high ideas, but the six-point charter from

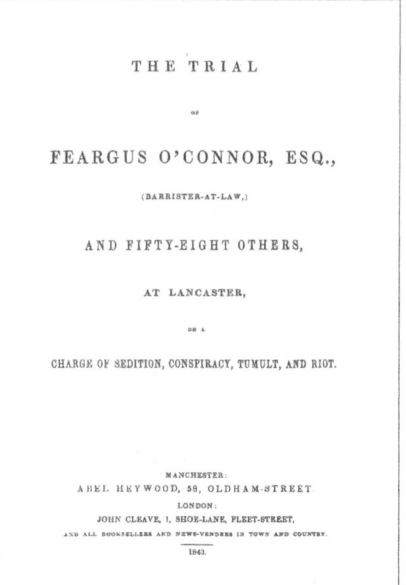

Trail account of O'Connor.

which the name comes made perfect sense at the time to all those English people who were excluded from having a vote. The charter included these points: universal suffrage (for adults), annual parliaments, vote by ballot, the abolition of the property qualification for MPs, payment of MPs and equal electoral districts.

The current practice before the 1832 Reform Act was that corruption was rife because 'pocket boroughs' were common seats, which were always won by the same family or party due to control of the voters or because of ridiculous situations in which some seats had only a handful of residents, who, of course, could easily be 'bought' as voters. Chartism, coming at a time when there were so many other privations, shortages, inequalities and injusticies evident in society, found a great deal of popular support.

An indication of that popularity came at the massive assembly at what is now Hartshead Moor, between Leeds and Bradford, in 1839. At the time it was known as Peep Green, and the Chartist rally there brought speakers such as poets, politicians and writers. The area was like a fair, with over 100 huts put up for the sale of food and drink. Some said that 500,000 people had turned up, but a more realistic figure was probably 200,000.

But for O'Connor, his focus of influence was to come first of all in print.

The Northern Star

By the mid-1830s O'Connor was preaching a list of what he called the 'Five cardinal points of radicalism', which related to the problems of poor relief – the factor that undoubtedly influenced the rise of Chartism. This followed an act in 1834 which meant that poor law guardians would stop relief to the 'able bodied' out of work who were outside their institutions. The dreaded workhouse would therefore become a kind of prison to

The Northern Star newspaper.

many – simply because they had to work and, of course, no national system of support existed, as we have now.

Leeds became the place where O'Connor saw the springboard for his idea and for the key communication channels between radicals that was so essential to success. His paper was *The Northern Star* and it began publication in 1837. As historians point out, the paper was not competitive with periodicals that were not stamped: he had to pay a stamp tax because of the format, and consequently it was too dear for the average labourer or factory worker. That did not stop its rise to influential prestige. The point is that it had substance: long reports of events were given and in-depth analysis. He had a team of correspondents who were paid, and he employed an editor to run the paper as he himself did not have that ability. He had William Hill doing that job, a true confirmed socialist and former minister in the Unitarian church. With him was Bronterre O'Brian, the leader-writer.

The new paper took up the cause of the Charter. Many middle-class Leeds men supported the cause as well – men like James Marshall, George Goodman and Samuel Smiles, the great self-help advocate. The Leeds Parliamentary Reform Association was created, with a statement of aims that ran 'to make the improvement in our political institutions, and the extension of the franchise to the great mass of people by all legal and constitutional means'. O'Connor had no time for it: he was moving towards a certainty that what became known as 'Physical Force Chartism' was the way forward.

Physical Force

The split in the Chartist is defined as the 'Moral Force' faction against the 'Physical Force' one. But O'Connor was not thinking in basic violent terms. He was coming to think that the ruling establishment would only give concessions if they feared something. He therefore wanted the demand for change to seem fearful and come across as a real substantial presence in politics, not a flash in the pan but the equivalent to a small-scale food riot. After all, yielding to those six points of the charter meant a relinquishment of massive power. So why should they do that? In *The Northern Star*, O'Connor called the 'moral force' approach 'moral humbug'. But he did make concessions.

The great historian G.D.H. Cole sums up the O'Connor situation like this: 'To a man of O'Connor's temperament, such an evasion came easy. No one, least of all O'Connor himself, knew till quite late in the day whether he was in favour of an appeal to force or not.'

By November 1839 the government had to act against leaders who seemed a potential threat, because there had been a serious rising in Newport, South Wales. O'Connor was arrested for seditious libel and put in York Castle. He managed to smuggle out an account of life inside the gaol for publication in Leeds in the *Star*. There was no keeping the man down: out of prison in 1841 he embarked on a long and demanding speaking tour.

As the decline came, even William Hill was arrested in Leeds. As the Charter failed and nothing was done to engage with the reforms suggested, and the establishment played for time, O'Connor moved on.

The End

As O'Connor became more and more frantic and desperate, he eventually had a clash in the House of Commons with the Leeds banker Becket Denison, MP for the West Riding. He was taken out of the House and later defined as insane, actually being taken to be confined in an asylum in Chiswick. He came out in 1854, went to live with his sister for a while, but then he died in 1852. Leeds had been the place where, in the ascendancy of his radical career, things had seemed optimistic. But reform was certainly not to come in his life time. For instance, secret ballots did not arrive until 1872.

Maybe Feargus O'Connor will go down in the records as a hero and a villain in Leeds.

TWELVE

The Dripping Riots, 1865

'His rash fierce blaze of riot cannot last'
(Shakespeare)

There were times in the Victorian period when, in spite of the usual demands of the law and the innate sense of the importance of order and peace, the much distressed working class just found it too much to tolerate when an injustice was seen to be done.

In some cases it was about the price of corn; other disturbances were in response to the heavy hand of the law being so heavy that it has offended decency and reason. But then there were other causes of terrible acts of rebellion and destruction that stemmed from something very small – like dripping, for instance.

Dripping has long had a place in the Yorkshire cooking repertoire, and older Leeds people will still talk fondly of their youth, when society was less health conscious and a treat was a dripping sandwich, salty, rich and satisfying. Back in 1865 dripping had dozens of uses for the woman of the house feeding her usually large family, and, in the case of domestic servants, taking a little dripping from the cooking done for the employer was common practice and generally accepted. But not so in the household of Henry Chorley in Park Square. On this occasion, in February of that year, he refused to follow that common practice.

Eliza Stafford gets no Dripping

Eliza, 50 years old, was Chorley's cook, and when she roasted a joint for him she expected the dripping to take home. Chorley was a powerful man in the city: a magistrate and also a respected surgeon. But respect went out of the door on this occasion. It was when Eliza was sent to Armley Gaol for the offence of taking the dripping that the trouble started. She was convicted of stealing two pounds of the stuff and given one month's imprisonment.

She was quite new to his employment, having been there for only a few months, living in. When challenged about the matter, she said that she was allowed it 'as a perquisite though I said nothing about that perquisite when I was first engaged to do the work'.

All hell broke loose around Chorley's place. What had happened to make things worse was that her trial had been held in camera, and the Mayor of Leeds himself had been on the bench. The spark was lit, so to speak, by an article in a paper, as a report at the time noted:

> 'In a few days after the committal of the woman attention was called to the case, in a spirit of indignation, by one of the local papers which is best known for its publication of sensational stories and in its indulgence of caricature sketches of local personages...'

The report also noted that newsboys were shouting out scraps of gossip and jokes, and that people were chatting about the affair in disgust; in the street this rhyme was heard:

> 'Now all you cooks and servant girls wot's very fond of tipping
> Don't take your master's scraps of fat and boil 'em down for dripping:
> For if you do bear this in mind, the magistrates won't fail
> To try you in a private court and send you off to gaol.'

The Campaign Intensifies

Time passed and then graffiti appeared on the walls of the Chorley home and on plenty of other walls, with such words as 'A month's imprisonment for 2lbs of dripping.' Then things escalated so that Chorley was vilified in the street and indeed harassed and bullied. He received threatening letters, and then placards began to appear expressing the view that Leeds people should assemble for a large celebration when Mrs Stafford came out of prison.

But before that, pressure mounted. A large and aggressive crowd gathered outside Chorley's house. At first they shouted insults, and then they threw missiles at the house, including snowballs and stones. Chorley had the courage to come out and face them; he tried to talk to them and explain his position on the matter but to no avail. They threw dirt at him. When the police arrived they gradually dispersed, but there was worse to come.

Late in the evening on 22 February a huge crowd assembled outside Armley Gaol expecting Mrs Stafford to appear, but she did not. The mob expected celebration but instead found that their friend was still locked up, or so they thought. In fact she had been let out earlier. After that the crowd were determined to go again to Chorley's house and this time they contrived to hang a bottle and an old dripping-pan to the end of a long pole. The police who stood by took a very long time to move the mob away.

Still the Leeds populace were not satisfied. The next day stones were thrown at the Chorleys' windows and the mob were pressing heavily on the forces of law. To make matters worse, the Chief Constable, Mr Bell, while trying to help move the crowd, fell heavily and dislocated a shoulder. The crowd mentality took over, and when people fell they were crushed and trampled. One man was under the feet of the mob and was so seriously injured he had to be taken to the infirmary. The police could not cope.

Enter the Military

The army at York were called for by telegraph, so by the evening men from the 8th Hussars were in Leeds. The authorities were not finished yet, because extra police from Bradford were called for as well. By 1865 the railways were well established so the soldiers travelled by train from York. There was a feeling of the riot being calmed by the time that the local journalists posted their reports, but late that night a crowd of about 2,000 gathered outside the town hall and shouted out insults. The police took the brunt of the anger as usual, and as this mob was moved away a stone cut deeply into the temple of one officer. There were several arrests, which was inevitable given the scale of destruction and lawlessness that had filled the city like a rising tide of rage.

Mrs Stafford was in Scarborough

All this time, Mrs Stafford had been elsewhere. She had left Leeds much earlier, going to Scarborough where her daughter lived. *The Times* man reflected that she showed good sense, 'preferring to avoid the questionable honours the crowd intended to confer upon her'. In other words, her appearance before her supporters would either have intensified the anger or made her a local hero. The politic action smacks of a reaction to sound advice from the police and prison governor. In the end, it was decided that the five men arrested should not be dealt with seriously. There was perhaps a feeling of regret for the mean and thoughtless use of power by a bench of three influential men of high status, with one woman in front of them and the Chorleys and other witnesses trailing into the town hall to condemn her. The newspapers had imagined and recreated that scene in the eyes of the public, and the formula was one for extreme disorder on the streets of Leeds.

We have to remember that the workers were one thing, but the so-called 'underclass' were another matter. Usually, when disorder hit the streets it was the lowest social order, desperate and pushed to the end of their tether by economic pressures such as the price of bread or the lack of jobs. But the Leeds dripping riots were, as far as we can gather, events in which decent people were goaded into militancy and sheer rage because of a terrible injustice against a decent working woman. In simple terms, it was a case of a confrontation between, on the one hand, the practice of goodwill and convention ('perks of the job') and, on the other hand, the letter of the law.

There was an element of absolute disgust at the immorality and injustice being shown by a man in high position. With hindsight, it is possible to say that the results of the street violence were partly a continuation of the old social convention of 'rough music', when a local wrongdoer was subject to torment and bullying for a moral 'crime', and it was also a case of total callousness on the part of a man who should have known better.

THIRTEEN

On Yer Bike in Victorian Leeds

'But you'll look sweet upon the seat
Of a bicycle made for two!'
(Harry Dacre)

In 1897 there was national concern over the clothing worn by ladies in the burgeoning cycle clubs across the land. The faction campaigning for 'rational costume' met at Oxford, and thousands waited for their arrival. As the cyclists rode around the town, reporters monitored the fact that crowds expressed disapproval of the attire. What the 'rational dress' supporters told the papers to aid their cause was that 'They were on the brink of a great danger, for if they could not get more people to support the rational dress the hideous costumes of skirts for cycling would become stereotyped in England.'

Basically, the good people of England were in a moral fit about 'bloomers' and suchlike modifications of dress.

In short, in late Victorian times cycling was so popular that it had the potential to divide opinion and become news, with burning issues of the day in its lifestyle. Manufacturers in Leeds had been a part of that flowering of the hobby since around 1870. Cycling clubs had been popular through the period into the Edwardian age.

1880 – Cycle Making Arrives

Leeds always was a great engineering centre, so when the call for bicycles came along the manufacturers were soon found. As cycling clubs

WHOLESALE & RETAIL CYCLE AGENT.

RIDING SCHOOL.

T. COOK,

COMMERCIAL BUILDINGS, PARK ROW

AND

27, THORNTON'S ARCADE,

LEEDS.

Plate 3 T. Cook: advertisement (*Jackson's Cyclists' Guide to York-shire, 1896*).

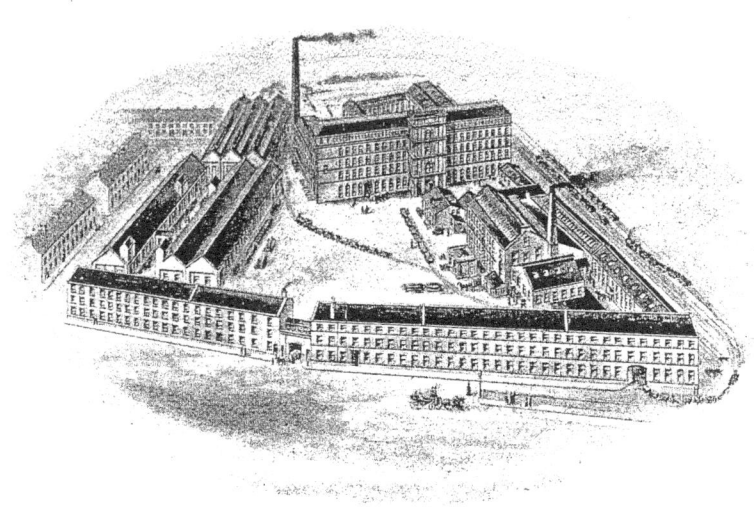

Plate 5(a) Yorkshire County Cycle Company Hunslet Factory (*Yorkshire Cycle Company Catalogue, 1899*).

Plate 5(b) The Hepworth Road Racer (*Yorkshire County Cycle Company Catalogue, 1899*).

Cycle adverts.

flourished, so the demand for bicycles increased again. By 1881 there were five cycle makers in the city, and it is logical that the people who started to build reputations in that industry already had ancillary skills that were called upon for the new machines. In other words, the technology base was there and all that was needed was adaptation and some business sense. A typical example was Thomas Bickerdyke Burnett, who was an ironmonger; his skills were quite easily applied to making bikes, and he did well.

Competition then played a part, as it always does, and the Airedale Bicycle Works in Park Lane proved successful, producing the cheapest machine in Leeds. Other firms realised that there was a lucrative market in providing repairs and maintenance rather than manufacture. The best way to understand what these companies were doing and what they offered is to consider the catalogues they produced, and there is a good example in one printed for Russom and Co. for 1883. In 1882 they were placed in North Street and made their main brand, the 'Special Leeds', with all kinds of slight specifications to appeal to different potential buyers.

Their very best *de luxe* bike was the 'high bicycle' – very dear at £15 – followed by models scaling down from £12 10 shillings to £6 and 10 shillings. Every firm needs good public relations and some advertising done with a little panache, and Russoms was no exception. They organised a bike ride from Leeds to Darlington in which a member of the Leeds Crescent Bicycle Club did the ride in just under 16 hours.

As with all fads, not only the product itself is sold but back-up services follow, such as tuition in how to ride the vehicles, such was the enterprising service given by Singer's company of Park Row. The tuition took place in a custom-made boarded area.

Walker Brothers

By the last decade of the 19th century the business had really expanded and there was a very wide choice of bicycles available for Loiners. There were the big firms, of course, but also a proliferation of small outfits. One street – New Station Street – was known as Bicycle Row in conversation. We tend to think that the term 'Acme' for any product has to be a joke, as used in Disney cartoons as a sad cliché of an unimaginative brand name. But the Acme Wheeleries did very well indeed in Leeds at Briggate in this period, but credit must be given to Walker Brothers of Meanwood Road and elsewhere. They really went into business on a grand scale, with 80 bikes for people to choose from, all on display at an exhibition in the town hall.

An advertisement of 1896, printed in the obscure *Yorkshire Owl Grand Cricket Annual*, shows a row of both men and women bikers lined up on show, with their machines, their cycling club board and logo above them. The information given is basic: just the name of the firm and their location, 'Junction of Meanwood Road and North Street'. But they also proudly describe their riding school as, 'Open to the public at all times. Efficient teachers always on hand to instruct and perfect pupils in the art of cycling.' Walkers even made the bikes for the Leeds City Police force. The management at Walkers had clearly thought about all aspects of the new leisure industry, and they saw it as exactly that – not as a fad or a crazy vogue. No doubt they thought long and hard about 'rational clothing', but their images used in adverts are very traditional and the women wear skirts and hats.

The Clubs

The Leeds clubs started in 1876 with the Leeds Amateur Bicycle Club (one wonders if there were *professional* riders); it was totally for the males of the city, and the middle class ones at that, certainly in the early phase up to around 1880. The Volante club had a specialism: members who were celebrities such as John Barran and Herbert Gladstone. But changes and adaptations had to come as the habit spread to others than merely the men, who would treat it as a proper sport and take it seriously. One of these developments, meeting demand, was the tricycle. Clubs at Harehills, Potternewton and Seacroft were quite early ones that lasted a long time and had a solid reputation.

Discussion in the press about the appeal of bikes to the young convey to us now the notion that a bicycle was 'cool' for the young. They just had to have one to be in the fashion.

Why did the leisure pursuit of cycling become so popular? The answers lie in the fact that the new machines were much safer than what had been on offer before. The 'Penny Farthing' was very hard to master and the early versions of bikes such as the velocipede, which was merely propelled by the feet, with no pedals, were a joke. Of course, there were different tyres for quite a while: some being pneumatic and some 'solids'. That was divisive, though sometimes in a jocular way. A typical club outing would be on a Saturday afternoon, and it must have been a blessed release for the pen pushers and shop workers to ride out to somewhere like Adel or Harewood to fill their lungs with fresh air. An account of a run by the Harehills club in 1884 includes facts such as the ride taking all day, going to Ledsham Park from Harehills, and they did not set off on the home run until eight in the evening, after 'a pleasant stroll through Ledsham park'. In addition, it was noted in the report that 'four members of the fair sex' were in the party.

Professionals
Of course, it seems to be in the British blood to step up from sheer fun to competitiveness, and cycling was no exception. In 1880 there was a professional race at Cardigan Fields off Kirkstall Road; a very sizeable crowd went along to this and the overall winner, cycling a phenomenal distance of over 1,000 miles, was F.J. Lees, who won himself the large sum of £50 for his efforts.

Some of the cycling stars from Leeds in this decade of the 'Naughty Nineties' were men like Albert Goodall, the man who founded the National Cyclists' Union, champion of Yorkshire riding and his vehicle was a design called the 'ordinary'. Another star was the mighty Summersgill – he won two West Riding Championships and the Yorkshire Mile Championship.

The Discovery of the Countryside
One of the really significant aspects of the cycling habit was the way it fitted in with the late Victorian and Edwardian discovery of the countryside for the masses of new commuters in the sprawling cities and new suburbs. So many novels and travel works of those days approach the question of how English people were hungering for knowledge of the country and the sense of freedom it offered. Books on those themes by writers such as Edward Thomas and Richard Jeffries had a large readership most of the time, and poems by the 'Georgian Poets' like de la

Mare and W.H. Davies also celebrated the Sunday jaunt into the country. In that setting, it is easy to see just what a deep impact cycling had on the opening up of 'park life' and rides to spots close to Leeds such as Knaresborough, with Mother Shipton's Cave, or to Temple Newsam.

Cycling was here to stay and most people saw that in the 1890s. It was cheap, healthy and sociable. It was to stay that way until the charabanc, and then the private motor cars stepped in to add a new fad. What must have surprised many is that it caused so much moral outrage. Through modern eyes, the leisure activity of cycling seems completely harmless, in the sense of being something which allows people to travel and escape their domestic round with ease and with fun. That is exactly what it was around 1890, but along with the new freedom came condemnation. Its development had been sudden really, with the term 'bicycle' first being used in 1868, and when the early so-called 'bone shakers' had been superseded by the new models, all kinds of social leisure openings came along for those people whose lives had previously been restricted by convention.

But the revolution came: the British Cycling Federation was formed in 1878 and such things as time trials came along, followed by cross-country biking. When the clubs went out into the country, it was only a matter of time before the welcome signs appeared on the inn walls: a CTC plaque of a wheel spoked with three wings. Some of these survive, one being in Yorkshire at Sykes House in Askrigg.

FOURTEEN

The Arcades Story

'A Nation of shopkeepers are very seldom so disinterested.'
(Samuel Adams)

In spite of all the changes that have made Leeds a city that looks towards modernity and global identity, there is still some persistently beautiful Victoriana inside the very centre, and the arcades are the jewel in the crown of that splendour.

The late 19th century was a time when, for the middle classes mostly, shopping was becoming as much a hobby as a necessity, and the nature of the shopping experience was considered by the businessmen who saw the established Victorian cities as places where, in addition to their workmanlike character, people came to wander and browse. From that impulse came the concept of the shopping arcade, and to walk along Briggate today is to see those wonderful creations as ornate and appealing as ever. It is almost as if the builders and artists of the 1870s and after had a very modern vision of how consumers would behave and what they wanted in the experience of going to town to shop.

A need had arrived for the consumer: amusement and leisure in between the busy affairs of either clerical work in town or when going down the shopping list and feeling the need to rest or slow down.

Charles Thornton and his Arcade

Much has been made of the compactness of the shopping centre of Leeds, and that is arguably the core of the success story: from The Headrow down to Boar Lane, the two main streets of Briggate and Vicar Lane and the off-streets provide most of the shopping in a limited area. A few decades ago, the main shops of Schofields, Lewis's, Boots (with its lending

Thornton's Arcade.

The inside of Thornton's Arcade.

library) and the Albion Street area had the main location of shops and public houses, providing the shopper with everything required. But crossing the main thoroughfares were and still are the arcades.

Charles Thornton made the first one where the Talbot Inn had its yard, in 1877–79. The clock has been the really fascinating element of a walk down that echoing but colourful few hundred yards of light and glass ever since that date. Generations of Leeds children, myself included c.1955, have walked into that arcade and been mesmerised by the tableaux scene of characters from Scott's story of *Ivanhoe*. The stock fabulous figures are there: Robin Hood, Friar Tuck and the rest.

The arcade is long and thin, stretching 74 by 4.5 metres; Gothic arches and high lancet windows go across the shop fronts. On the iron roof-trusses there are dragon figures, and those figures from Scott, created by J.W. Appleyard, dominate the view. The whole development around the arcade included the City Varieties (parallel to the Headrow and very close to it, and also offices that run alongside). As one enters from Briggate the effect is of brick and painted stone, with trios of lancet windows and columns between. At the entrance there is a chateau roof. The clock above the tableaux is by Potts (see the next chapter).

Frank Matcham and the County Arcade

In the Victoria Quarter, between Briggate and Vicar Lane, the architect Frank Matcham designed the County Arcade in what had been a meat market area. His concept was a three-block design with storeys and attic; the terracotta baroque gives this an air of quality and grand Augustan leisure. The arcade has a cast-iron roof and glazed domes; the female heads there symbolise the three notions of Liberty, Commerce and Justice.

Matcham was born in Torquay and was apprenticed to a surveyor before going to London to his first position with Jethro Robinson, where he married the boss's daughter, and when his father-in-law died, there was Frank, only 24, running the business. What became his special province in his profession was the building of theatres: more than 200 such places came from him and other colleagues. Some of the more famous ones are the Hackney Empire, the Wakefield Theatre Royal and London Palladium.

At the turn of the century he designed the Victorian Quarter, and the Empire Theatre was in the centre of that (demolished in the 1960s), but the County Arcade is very much as it always was. He had a love of elaboration, but his buildings have a marvellous symmetry and use of contrasting stone and brick. The appeal of his work is a creative fusion of exotic-seeming grandeur at the high levels and tasteful decoration elsewhere.

More of the Same

The Queen's Arcade was built in 1888–89, the Grand Arcade in 1896–98 and the Victoria Arcade (named after the queen at the Jubilee) in 1898. The Grand is done in renaissance style, made by Smith and Tweedale, with blue and yellow tiles at the entrances. The two arcades that run parallel here dissect Briggate and Vicar Lane. Inside there was at one time the Tower Cinema, and again a clock by Potts, showing Knights and castle doors.

George Smith (1782–1869), as well as his work in Leeds, produced some truly-famous buildings elsewhere, including the Cornhill entrance to the Royal Exchange, the Greenwich railway station and Gresham College in London.

Queen's Arcade.

Over the years, various companies have tried to set up their establishment there and most have worked hard to integrate with the required style. Leeds shoppers must lament the fact that some of these have fallen by the wayside (such as Pollard's café), but, on the other hand, Harvey Nichols now exists within the area of one arcade and that has to indicate a high esteem from the metropolis.

It is impossible to imagine Leeds centre without the arcades. Many famous writers and thinkers have reflected on the importance of the arcade in European communities, seeing the first ones, in the Victorian period, as indicative of that struggle to maintain the ornate beauty of Mediterranean Renaissance and Baroque architecture in the new utilitarian world of England, in the high summer of the Industrial Revolution – when the benefits of that long and hard effort towards a better quality of life for all was just bearing fruition.

FIFTEEN

Potts and his Clocks

'and then the clock collected in the tower
its strength, and struck...'
(A.E. Housman)

The Potts dynasty of clockmakers in Leeds goes back a long way – to 1776 in fact. In that year Robert Potts had his company going. He came south and settled in Bondgate; then his son William followed in the business. Their company at first concentrated on manufacturing flyers and spindles, but there was plenty for young William to learn and he was able to take up an apprenticeship: this was back in Darlington, where he worked for Samuel Thompson.

Potts in Pudsey
Back came William to the Leeds area and started in the employment of James Naylor, and there he made his first longcase clock. He lived with his father in Pudsey and he married in Calverley. It did not take long for the firm to expand, and in 1840 the aims were much more ambitious; in the first phase of the business, in addition to domestic clocks, the connections with the North East paid off and they had a regular line of orders for church clocks, set up in turrets.

After some effort, Potts found himself a colleague with talent in abundance. This was Edmund Denison, and the story handed down about this was that Denison was set on by the vicar of the church at Ilkley who wanted a new turret clock – his task to interview the man tendering for the work. It seems that a long line of men gave in and walked off without work, but Potts proved his deep knowledge and showed his enthusiasm to such a degree that he was engaged. Then Potts and Denison became workmates.

The Town Hall Clock and Others

The clock at Ilkley Parish Church was made and put in place, and following that triumph Potts and Dennison went from strength to strength in business. Michael Potts, in writing the family history, notes that between 1850 and 1855 they made the clocks for churches in Burley, Farsley, Yeadon and Tong. As they scaled upwards and worked with another true craftsman, Edward Dent, there was a long saga to come regarding the clock placed in Leeds Town Hall (completed in 1858). Potts began work on that clock in 1860. It had been designed and made by Dent, but there were problems: the winding and regulating mechanisms were not right.

Potts and two other men worked solidly to try to put this right, persevering for two months before their masters finally had enough and intervened, suggesting that Denison should give them some fresh guidance. Denison was sure that working through the night and concentrating on specific alterations would sort it all out, but there was a hex on the whole operation, as a lifting hammer line snapped. 1861 brought no progress; in fact the clock was now functioning, but the problem then was that it stopped every hour on the minute before the strike. Two further months of hard work followed. Continuing work made it certain that the whole thing was changing from being a clock made by Dent to a Potts clock.

But Potts won in the end. He then moved on to work all over Yorkshire, from Thorne to Bradford and from mills to chapels. In comparison to the travails over the Leeds Town Hall clock, the work they did in making and positioning the clock for the Bradford parish church was fine and problem-free: they made a Cambridge quarter-chiming clock for that. Leeds centre then became Potts's new base – in the Headrow. If nothing else, he could regularly monitor the Town Hall Clock from there, as he was close enough to step outside and stare at it.

Guildford Street

The new headquarters was close to Butts Court and Green Dragon Yard. The orders came in regularly and perhaps the most prestigious one was the job of replacing the old (1826) stable clock at Roundhay Park mansion. He was well paid for this and the whole concern was thriving. Cuthbert Brodrick, who had designed the Leeds Town Hall, also worked on the Corn Exchange by the Calls, and Potts was called on to supply the clock there. So successful was

A clock made by Potts in Thornton's Arcade.

the firm that the sons were being nurtured to become involved, and they did so prominently after William had a bad accident in 1866; he had a bad fall and was lucky not to be very severely injured, but he was left with a weakened constitution to a certain extent. Robert became a partner the next year.

The new publicity for the firm was worded 'William Potts and Son'. There were two other sons coming along: James and Joseph. William was to need all the help he could get, because he won some major orders as time went on. The Potts reputation was stunningly good: the work stood there as evidence of quality for all to see.

Major Orders across the Country

The clocks were now being placed in projects done by the most famous artists and designers in England, like the clock for Sir Gilbert Scott's Preston Town Hall. The family historian considers that to have been 'the first prestigious order', but this seems to underplay the earlier achievements.

Others of a high standing flowed, such as the clock for the Bradford Wool Exchange. The firm even replaced one of its own clocks – the one made and installed in Burley in 1850, replaced in 1870. This was all hard labour and it took remarkable strength to do this installation work. The story that best illustrates this is the placing of a clock in the Winter Gardens; the object had a diameter of four feet and was to be positioned 30 feet from the ground. As Michael Potts has explained:

'This meant that the clock, in complete form, had to be taken up two long ladders, and fixed about 30 feet above ground level…He managed to do it with the help of his joiner and foreman. Robert was a strong man in his youth and capable of lifting weights far in excess of his own body weight of ten and a half stones…'

The arcade clocks then followed, including one in the Imperial Arcade in Birmingham and, of course, the Leeds arcade clocks.

Williams's Death

William had a fall at home, going down some steps with no handrail to hold. He broke his leg and battered his head very painfully. He was, after all, 77 years old, and it was a profound blow to his system. He had had the severe fall earlier, of course, as well. William died on 7 January 1887 and the local paper gave a glowing obituary. His biographer has said that '…there is no question that William Potts was an outstanding engineer who took advantage of the Victorians' desire for expansion and for creating buildings for which they will always be remembered.'

Personally, one feels that he must have had sleepless nights about the ill-fated Leeds Town Hall clock, and any man who overcame those obstacles has to command respect. Like Christopher Wren's epitaph, we only have to ask people looking at Potts's heritage to 'look around them' to see the evidence.

Of course, all this industry came at a price. That was usually in the living conditions of the workers. James Smith, writing a report in 1845, had this to say on the 'Filthy Yards of Leeds':

'By far the most unhealthy localities of Leeds are close squares of houses, or yards, as they are called, which have been erected for the accommodation of working people. Some of these, though situated in comparatively high ground, are airless from the enclosed structure, and being wholly unprovided with any form of under-drainage, or convenience, or arrangement for cleansing, are one mass of damp and filth…'

Progress, it seems, had to come with a high cost for the ordinary people.

SIXTEEN

Tetley's, a Leeds Icon

'For a quart of ale is a dish for a king.'
(Shakespeare)

For someone growing up in Leeds in the 1960s, the Tetley huntsman was indicative of something essentially of and from the heart of Yorkshire. That may seem like a pathetic cliché, but the fact is that the centre of Leeds was then packed with Tetley pubs and the red-coated huntsman evoked good living, celebration and something very English. It can come as a shock to Leeds folk to see the huntsman in other towns, over other pubs.

Joshua Tetley the maltster was around in 1822, but it was in 1834 that the second Joshua opened his brewery. Tetley and Son appeared in 1839. They abandoned the wines and spirits trade to concentrate on making beer, and it was an age of beer shops and also gin drinking for the poor and the working classes. He had no trouble finding customers. Joshua died in 1859 and his son Francis took over.

In 1874 Tetley were selling over 160,000 barrels of ale a year, and in 1890 they branched out into running retail trade in brewery-owned pubs. The pub took over from the beer shop as the working men discovered a wider leisure habit, embracing pub games and also involving themselves in the working men's clubs across Yorkshire.

Tetley's brewery from an 1893 collection.

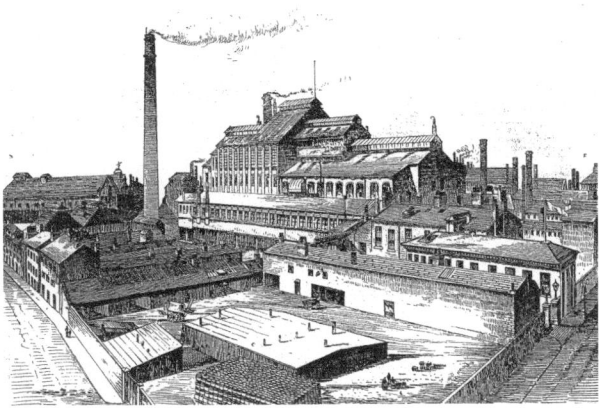

'The Largest Brewery in the West Riding'

In 1893 an enterprising publisher gave the world a massive celebration of Yorkshire business, and he described Tetley's in Leeds, showing a detailed engraving of the brewery in Hunslet Road, with surrounding wall and huge buildings behind the chimney and sheds, as a fortress almost, like a small kingdom within the city.

Francis Tetley had died in 1893, and the book notes that the personnel of the firm at that time included 'Mr C. Ryder, Mr C.F. Tetley and Mr C.F. Ryder who trade its entirety.'

The book also explains the heart of the quality achieved:

> 'Almost the whole of the malt used by the firm is made in their various maltings both within and outside the brewery yard. Wells on the premises ensure a never-failing supply of excellent water, while boreholes several hundred feet deep furnish that required for cooling...Cask cleaning is done by special machinery which renders the heading and unheading of the casks unnecessary.'

In other words, they had streamlined and refined the essential components of production.

At that time they employed 500 workers (or 'hands', as they were then called); they were not merely in Leeds either, because they had stores in London at St Pancras, at Slater Street in Liverpool and at Jackson's Row in Manchester.

In Yorkshire they also had a network of bases for distribution, covering Scarborough, York, Filey, Holmfirth, Hull, Knaresborough, Sowerby Bridge and Ripon. In the 1890s Tetley's were producing all the varieties for which they have remained famous ever since, principally: pale ale, bitter, mild, stout and porter.

The brewery was built in 1853, and between that date and the end of the century Tetley's constantly enlarged and improved; the original site of the first brewery, by the 1890s, was covered merely by the fermenting room and hop stores. Around that stood six acres of land. A new malthouse was built in 1866 and the advertisements at that time were proud to proclaim that the brewery worked 'Under the personal supervision of the principals who are well known and much esteemed in the district of Leeds, and who closely adhere to the honourable and straightforward methods that have always characterised the dealings of their house...'

Houdini in the Beer Cask

In 1911 the great Harry Houdini, famous escapologist and magician, was booked for a show at the Empire Theatre in Briggate. As was his practice to add some hype to the occasion, he challenged anyone around the city to set up a situation that would be so dire that he would be trapped. By that time, Houdini had moved from the small-time shows in travelling fairs in America to top-billing across the world, and his challenge was really top-notch media public relations for the showman.

Houdini in the beer cask.

Tetley's responded, as they knew that he was fond of being submerged in liquid, restrained, and set the task of escaping in a short time. They set the challenge of an escape from a massive beer cask full of bitter, and he relished that. But it was one of the great man's failures. It was not the padlocks that defeated him but the stink of the beer. As he was a teetotaller who was troubled with the inhalation of beer fumes, he was in great difficulty and nearly drowned. This was on 9 February, and he was dragged from the cask in a severely troubled state.

The famous illusionist took it hard as he was accustomed to winning and being the darling of the crowds.

Benefactors and Profits

Of course, the form of Tetley's did extremely well, rising to a very high status. In 1928 it advertised stock to become a public limited company and the share capital then was in an issue of £500,000, 5.5 percent redeemable debenture. It was floated and forms printed in *The Times*.

The substantial profits had made the owners very rich, but the Ryders and Tetleys were liberal with their money and very public-spirited; in 1902, when Charles Ryder died, he left a personal estate of almost £428,000 net, and it was stated in the newspaper reports that he 'authorised the executors to allow a piece of land to be used for the purposes of St Michael's Church, in Crown-Point Road, Leeds.' Similarly, Mr C.F. Tetley lived to the grand-old age of 85, and at his death in 1934 he had attained the status of a VIP in Leeds, being Lord Mayor of the city and having the 'Freedom of the City' given to him in 1926. He could have been made a baronet, but he turned that honour down. Like others in his family, he gave freely, donating £20,000 to Leeds University. He regularly gave money to charities and churches.

The success of the company has been phenomenal; in 1950 Tetley's owned 500 pubs and in 1961 they became partners with Ind Coope and Ansells, forming the organisation of Allied Breweries. Modernity and technology have, naturally, transformed the brewery business, and in May 1989 the latest version of their brewery opened, but still very close to the early 19th-century brewing house. Since 1993 the world has known them as 'Carlsberg-Tetley'.

But the usual deep interests in the history and imagery of the company go on: the huntsman image attracts all kinds of collectors, for instance. In 1981 Tetley issued a set of matchboxes and these are now collectables. In addition to that public image is the traditional Leeds city centre Tetley pub; entirely typical of that identity is the Ship, nestling up a ginnel from Briggate. That and many more like it evoke a memory of Leeds long gone, but it is easy to imagine the ghosts in those taprooms and saloons. For generations of Leeds drinkers, the Tetley name and the huntsman are as profoundly a part of Leeds as Elland Road football ground and the Kirkgate market.

Of course, the beer-drinking habit is one thing, but the pub as a centre for local recreation is quite another. The old photographs of Leeds,

particularly around the bridge and the Calls and by the canal, show an area of cheap beer shops. That was quite enough for many working men – just to have beer for solace and to ease the pains of physical labour. It took much longer for the pub to become a sociable place where games were played and thoughts shared. Tetley's can say with pride that they played a part in that quiet but important process from gin and beer shop at the street corner to the centre of conviviality.

The Ship.

SEVENTEEN

A Team of Victorian Businessmen

'I want nothing but what is severely workful.'
(Charles Dickens)

Leeds has always been renowned for its engineering. In Victorian Leeds there were plenty of those companies, but also a formidable array of other industries as well. By the end of the 19th century Leeds could boast substantial establishments of manufacture in soap, watches, clothing, tool making, wool, paper, ironfounding, flax spinning, preserves, leather, beer, oil and glass. But clothing and engineering have been high on the list and were so in the early years of the Industrial Revolution.

The Engineers

There were engineers and tool makers for all purposes and markets, but the really large-scale ones are represented by Joseph Hall of the Burley Engine Works. Hall established his business in 1872, and he expanded gradually until, by the end of the century, he had over an acre and a line of three main sheds. His place was crammed full with engines and cranes, and drilling, slotting and planing machines. A summary of the firm after 21 years of work included the information that Hall's had 'just completed a large contract for an overhead railway for one of the largest corporations in the country'. They also dealt in second-hand machinery. Typical machines made by Hall were the band knife-splitting machine and the item sold as 'Hall's Premier Striking-Out and Setting Machine'.

Another very successful firm was Tannett Walker of Hunslet. Benjamin Walker, magistrate and local celebrity, died in 1891, and Arthur Tannett Walker and Major Frederick Walker took over near the end of Victoria's reign. They employed over 1,000 workers, and

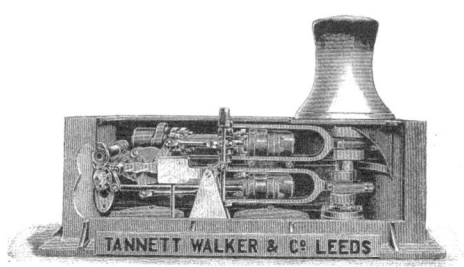

Tannett Walker – a typical product.

their reputation was always high. One of their specialities was the hydraulic forging press, which they made for the German giants Krupp and for the John Brown firm of Sheffield. They also installed plant at steelworks, and it was commented at the time that 'Their Bessemer and Siemans-Martin steel plant is regarded as unsurpassed...and they stand in the very front rank as makers of such important plant as rail, plate, cogging and corrugating mills.'

Tannett Walker excelled in making the really heavy, powerful items in the engineering repertory: such things as steam hammers and hydraulic railway capstans. Their forging press was immense and solid, standing at a weight of 350 tons. They even supplied machinery for dockyards and at the Woolwich Arsenal.

Engineering in Leeds in the Victorian years cannot be described without a mention of Joseph Barron's company, a corn mill engineer. The

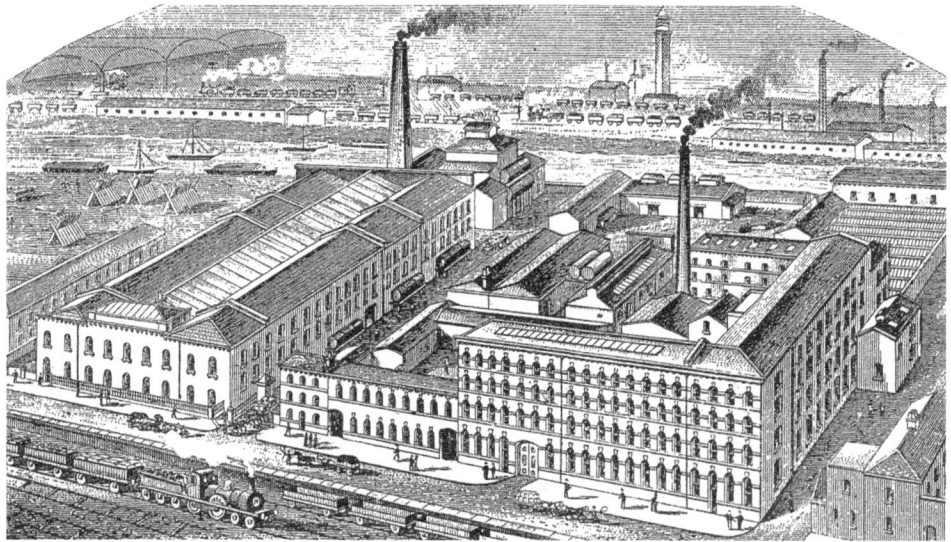

Whitehall Soap Works.

catalogue says it all, 'The firm are large manufacturers of such appliances for corn mills and roller mills, centrifugal purifiers, scalpers, rotary sieves', as well as 100 other items.

Specialisms for Every Need

Late Victorian Leeds was also the place where people and companies could purchase a whole range of things made for very specific purposes relating to the changing lifestyles at that time, at the height of empire, and when the new commuter class in the cities was expanding and changing the nature of the middle-class buyer and householder. A good example of this domestic ware is the firm of Joseph Ross at Wellington Street. Ross made their garments at the Airedale Mills in Armley, making 'fancy woollen and worsted clothing'. Their notes on the business at this period state that they had 'a considerable proportion of their productions' finding their way to 'London markets'.

John Atha was also in this category: an expert in producing leather goods from his works in Orchard Road, Hunslet. He formed his works in 1863 and began to specialise in making 'velvet chamois', but the firm is a classic example of what Victorian businesses had learned from the start – to make products from waste and from by-products of the main product. In the process of making the velvet chamois, Atha saw that he was creating a good stock of 'sod oil' – this being the mixture of cod oil and grease. Its use was in softening leather and so would be bought by leather curriers.

Another boom industry in that century was waste paper. Men became millionaires by using and reusing waste materials, and William Benson of the Quarry Hill Paper Works was typical of this. He was most interested in making felt-paper, and in the process of using the waste he came up with a useful invention for the paper trade as a whole – the beater plate, something no sooner conceived than snapped up by Rawsons of Union Mills. It was a way of producing paper in which, as he claimed, 'Time and power are saved and uniformity of pulp is secured.'

Hunslet had always been an engineering centre, ever since the acceleration of powered production; in 1871 there were almost 200 puddling furnaces there. In 1889 the steelworks in Leeds produced more tram rails than anyone else. Later munitions became big business of course, but the real importance in this period in terms of manufacture is the logistics of how all the elements were put together – business acumen, technical knowledge and good advertising and marketing.

Clothing Trade

This survey would not be complete without mention of the clothing industry. The last years of the 19th century saw the proliferation of middle-sized firms concentrating on particular garments or types of cloth. For example, Clough and Ramsden made 'fancy trousers' and 'worsted clothing'. They were doing what many did in a place where they had plenty of machinists and cutters: target markets within certain industries, so that commercial and industrial clothing became their forte.

Hartley and Co, of Canal Street, was an ambitious and 'modern' outfit, with an eye for trends and fads; they made 'stylish dress fabrics' and 'marvels of the season', as their adverts proclaimed. They went into detail when they described what they had on offer, explaining patterns in this way: 'Tweeds in the new Knop designs, plaid tweeds and stuffs, snowflake tweeds, twist tweeds, beiges, summer serges, cashmeres, the new Bengaline dress tweeds etc.'

The ready-made clothing business went on in 1,000 little workshops; this was to continue as a staple until well into the 20th century, and even in the 1950s and 1960s there was still a thriving, lucrative proliferation of small firms that existed through piecework and also by outwork, as a strange prolongation of the old 18th-century domestic industry. A typical Leeds clothing firm would be of medium size, either in the industrial-domestic suburbs like Beeston or in the centre around Sheepscar, and it would depend for a long time on non-unionised labour, long hours and the allure of piecework.

The Negatives

Naturally, all that industry and manufacture took its toll on the population. There was a long-standing problem with public health in Victorian Leeds. The companies exploiting the cheap and available labour and the ideal geographical position of the city at first had little awareness of or education about pollution and noxious smells. A poem of 1857 by William Osburn sums up the issue:

'The AIRE below is doubly dyed and damned;
The AIR above, with lurid smoke is crammed;
The ONE flows steaming foul as Charon's Styx,
It's poisonous vapours in the other mix.'

It took a great deal of patience and a long line of reformers to sort this out and make public health a priority. But for most Victorians the industry was fine – it paid them wages and they put up with the side-effects. Leeds, like so many other English towns and cities, had its industry at a price – in human terms, very high.

EIGHTEEN

Berkeley Moynihan, Surgeon

'He had always had a natural flair and fondness for anatomy.'
(Donald Bateman)

Berkeley Moynihan, who was to become Lord Berkeley Moynihan with stacks of letters after his name, is, without doubt, one of the heroes of Leeds who is barely known to people of the city. He was born in Malta and his family always had military connections; his father had won the Victoria Cross at the siege of the Redan in the Crimean War, killing five Russians in hand-to-hand fighting, and he later served with distinction in the Indian Mutiny. Naturally, young Berkeley went to Sandhurst, but it was not for him: he was cut out to be a doctor, and he started his studies at the Leeds School of Medicine in 1883, graduating in 1887.

He was the most successful British surgeon of the Edwardian period, specialising in surgery of the stomach, gall bladder and intestines. At the time he was learning his profession, the whole abdomen was rarely explored surgically; it was only done in extreme emergencies and almost always ended in the death of the patient. But there was more to Moynihan than his medical specialism. He was prominent in World War One, and in later life he became a public figure of great

Berkeley Moynihan.

authority, speaking before the most respected and high-ranking people in society. He was a sociable, charismatic figure. In his obituary, it was said that 'Moynihan was wholly incapable of holding a subordinate position. He was a born leader, and he enjoyed the fame, both professional and public, for which he had not long to wait. It became usual for surgeons from all parts of the world to visit Leeds General Infirmary to watch his methods...'

Clarendon Road, the surgeon's home.

The Medical Man

In the years just after he qualified, Moynihan did many things, as a person early in a career tends to do. He was self-supporting and made a little money from his private practice, but he had to be a freelance and work with what we call today 'a wide portfolio'. This extended to assisting the top surgeon Mr Jessop and working as the prison surgeon for Leeds, looking after the health care element in prison. But this also meant a duty he hated: he had to be present at every execution in Armley. But, as his biographer Donald Bateman has said, there were deep satisfactions, even early on:

'Lastly, he was paid for the work he did as one of the official teachers of anatomy in the Yorkshire College, to which position he was raised in 1894. That work gave him great pleasure; he had always had a natural flair for anatomy, and early recognised the supreme importance of its detailed knowledge to the surgeon.'

His first cases involved a wound below an eye, gout, spinal tuberculosis and many others. His very first operation was the drainage of a suppurating gland in the groin. The whole treatment involved 11 visits and plenty of dressings, and it cost the patient 35 pounds and 11 shillings.

In 1893 he passed the examination to become a Master of Surgery and was house surgeon at Leeds. Then he became Professor of Clinical Surgery in 1909. He was knighted in 1912.

Moynihan travelled across the world to learn more about his chosen profession from the experts in the fields, and, although he was a learned and dedicated man, his attitudes to patients and peers was always sensitive and open-minded. The Hippocratic credo that 'the patient comes first' always counted for something with him. He was so impressive and successful that his fame spread far beyond Leeds. He became the first provincial surgeon to be elected to the Royal College of Surgeons. He came to realise that England was not keeping up with the developments in surgery elsewhere; he also saw that there was no cross-current and free flow of information between the surgeons and hospitals that were across oceans. Communication in that context had countless benefits for all concerned, and Moynihan's remedy was to found a journal that would act as a focal point for knowledge and research. This became the *British Journal of Surgery*, which had a group of surgeons relate together as a kind of club. Moynihan was in his element in clubs and professional gatherings all his life.

In the War

When World War One began in 1914 he was the ideal person to hold a senior position in the army, and he was made the main consultant surgeon to the Northern Command. With a rank of Major-General, he served on the Western Front and with the British Expeditionary Force. This was at a time when medical work in the army concentrated on the body rather than the mind, so illnesses related to neurasthenia and battle stress would have been marginal concerns for him – he mended limbs and entered the abdomen to work on organs. His work was therefore extremely stressful for him, continuing under pressure and with a massive number of casualties every day. But the positive side to this is that it was a great learning experience for the surgeon, and the war years were invaluable to him in that respect.

The Professional Figurehead

In a letter to *The Times* in 1923 Moynihan makes it clear that he was the foremost representative of his profession at the time, writing about the definition and standing of surgery. In the course of that letter he explained the element in his work that is not often expressed, 'The practice of clinical surgery makes a further heavy demand upon qualities of temperament and of character which are little exercised in the cloistered tranquillity of the laboratory.' That was one side of his work well explained, the other was the issue of what general practising surgeons were achieving in comparison with the 'scientific' achievements of researchers. But there are physicians and surgeons whose lives have been spent in the wards and in the operating theatres of our hospitals, whose contributions to 'scientific' medicine are entitled to rank with this (academic work).

In other words, in later life Moynihan had taken on the role of public educator, distinguished speaker and spokesman. If the press wanted an opinion or a comment on a topical medical issue, they went to Berkeley Moynihan.

For instance, in 1927 he delivered the Hunterian Oration before the Royal College of Surgeons, and he took that opportunity to summarise the success story of surgery in Britain, talking about the attitudes previous to the changes brought about by the great Lister. Before then, hospitals had been 'Houses of death', he noted. Moynihan always practised Listerian methods, and in that lecture he explained that it was Lister who had made hospital surgery work free from risk. In the 1920s, said Moynihan, surgeons went to work 'in a frame of mind completely unknown to their ancestors'. He also made the important point in that lecture of a holistic view, stating that surgery could only advance if it learned from and related to

Woodhouse Square.

such areas of medical knowledge as bacteriology, physics and physiology. He was talented, with an epigram saying 'The physiologist too, should stand by the bedside; there are many things he can learn better from men than from mice.'

In addition to the speaking and expression of opinions, Moynihan wrote a medical bestseller: *Abdominal Operations*. It was typical of the man to have done that, as he was a meticulous writer in everyday practice, leaving detailed notes on cases from the very beginning.

Honours

Berkeley Moynihan became Baron Moynihan of Leeds in 1929. Leeds gave him the honorary freedom of the city and the university made him vice-chancellor in the jubilee year of 1924. Honours constantly came his way, and he reached the status of a well-known public figure. Few men attain that place in which their portrait is painted and hung at the 'Headquarters' of a profession, but Moynihan did – his portrait being painted by Richard Jack, RA, and presented to the Royal College of Surgeons. His number of honorary degrees was 14, maybe a record.

Lord Berkeley Moynihan died on 7 September 1936 at his home at Carr Manor, Meanwood, in Leeds, aged 71. His son, Patrick, became a barrister, no doubt inheriting some of Moynihan's charisma and dedication to his career.

NINETEEN

The Coroner's Tales

'A man of fine presence, dignified and shrewd.'
(*The Leeds Mercury*)

Generally, the man in the street knows little of what goes on at a coroner's court. But the word 'inquest' is there in all the legal and criminal case books in print. Sometimes these courts were held in pubs and inns, sometimes in local halls and mansions. But at the centre was the coroner – a man with a sacred and important duty. He made the first decision, for centuries, regarding the next stage in a homicide investigation.

In the years before forensic science, the scene would have been something like this: a man's wife lies dead in a street outside a pub. The couple have been seen arguing and the man has, on occasion, been seen to be violent. But the woman has a reputation as well, and there are known lovers on the scene. She has been found dead, but no one is sure whether she collapsed through too much drink and cracked her head, if she had a serious illness affecting her brain or if she was battered with a blunt instrument. All this comes before the poor coroner, who has to take medical statements and testimony from anyone else involved.

At first, all such courts were held with a jury, but since 1927 a coroner's jury has only been needed in a few inquest cases, and usually the coroner sits by himself. Nowadays a jury is only essential when the death has been in prison, in police custody, a case reportable by the Health and Safety Executive or in circumstances prejudicial to public safety.

All that modern vocabulary would have been lost on the coroner for Leeds in the late Victorian and Edwardian period, John Cooper Malcolm. Malcolm was of Scottish origin but was born in Leeds. He was elected coroner in 1876 and was to hold that office until 1923. He was the oldest coroner in England, and he saw surely every variety of death possible in the Leeds of those boom and bust years, between the arrival of the new industries to World War One and the aftermath.

Malcolm was highly respected in his profession, being president of the Coroners' Society of England and Wales, and he had worked on an amazingly high number of 25,000 inquests (which is a conservative estimate). He had the particularly unpleasant duty of being coroner for Armley Gaol and held 50 inquests on murderers there, including that of the famous Charlie Peace. His background qualified him well for that role, as he was a solicitor, and he had vast experience of the work the role entailed as he learned from a Mr Barrett, who had been deputy to a former coroner in Leeds.

Earlier inquests had been in public houses, and when he retired Mr Malcolm described these events:

> 'Publicans…were usually at great pains to make a coroner's jury
> comfortable, and the most that the innkeepers in Leeds got was a
> fee of five shillings for their trouble. Certain it is that in the old-
> fashioned inns, juries were made more comfortable than they
> sometimes are in vestries and school rooms where the inquests
> have been held since.'

Malcolm, a solid-looking man with a full beard and a tough, no-nonsense expression, was widowed twice and left a large fortune. He was described by a colleague as having a 'cool, calm, judicious and judicial mind'.

The Cases: Suicides

The deaths Malcolm had to handle were mostly those one might expect from the kind of people in a city undergoing huge social change; the pressures of hardship, unemployment, or, conversely, long and exhausting working hours, moral problems, legal stresses and, of course, mental illness all became factors in the coroners' courts. At the basis of it all was the 'suspicious death', and the stories of the deaths make gripping human tales in those dark and dangerous years.

Suicides were some of the commonest categories of course. Many were women, most of whom took their own lives because of problems relating to childbirth, prostitution or drink. A fairly typical case is that of Mary

Ann Brooke, only 19 years of age, in 1885. Mary was the daughter of the manager of York Street Gasworks. What was typical in the case is that her mother reported at the inquest that the girl had been 'low and moody…though she had no reason to believe that she was insane', as the *Yorkshire Post* reported. But what was much less common was the gruesome part of the tale: that at first a woman's leg was found, then later the rest of her. The police surgeon explained that the injuries were caused when she fell into the canal and hit something very hard.

But all was not explained: a sister stated that Mary had in fact had mental problems, and that her mind had been 'unhinged' for some time. The result was probably what coroners dislike – an open verdict.

Sometimes, suicides were not a simple case of a person drowning themselves or slitting their wrists. In 1856 a man called James Foreman of Sussex Street, who was a wood carver by occupation, acted as treasurer to one of those Victorian institutions, a Friendly Society. He found that the accounts did not balance and, clearly thinking that fingers would point at him, these doubtful thoughts led to a state of mind so extremely distraught that he was considered to be, as the inquest stated, 'temporarily insane', and he tried to cut his own throat. His first attempt failed, so of course he was watched closely, but one day he walked into the office where his colleagues were working with blood spewing from him. He leaned over a basin and the blood from his throat filled it.

He was asked how he had done the dreadful deed, and he explained

Cooper Malcolm, Coroner.

that he had used a razor, there it was beside him. There are many very sad and tragic aspects to that case: one being that he left several children behind, and the other being that, as it turned out, the society's funds were perfectly in order and the books balanced.

Many suicides were drownings, such as that of a man who remained anonymous (as many did), found in the canal at Monk Bridge and taken to the Wellington Inn in Wellington Street. All we know is that he was about 35, five feet three inches tall and he wore tweed.

But more detailed and also quite common is a suicide from 1866, caused mainly by a gambling habit. Samuel Birchall worked for the Midland Railway; he had worked for the firm for 20 years, and he was 55 at the time. He was, as the newspaper put it, 'strongly addicted to the turf' and was of 'very dissipated habits'. He was quite a character, with a shop as well as a job, and a house in Sheffield as well as in Leeds. At first he was found totally drunk, and then he was heard to say that he was tired of the world. What happened after that was something all families dread when a member is under such mental duress. He told them that he had 'taken something' – he had, in fact, taken opium, and he had 'taken enough to do for himself'. The medical men tried a stomach pump but it was too late.

The verdict was '*felo de se*' – an important category of suicide, meaning self-murder and so a felony. As the death was before the 1870 Forfeiture Act, it meant that he would lose goods and possessions. Of course, that was immaterial, as he had gambled away virtually everything.

Cases: Mystery

Some deaths are completely mysterious, of course, as in the example of John Rider of Briggate in 1855. His body was found on a Tuesday morning near the Bowling tunnel on the Lancashire to Yorkshire Railway. His corpse was terribly mutilated as it was lying across the rails. His head and face had been dissected – the people arriving to see this needed strong stomachs, for sure. The first to do so was a man called Pearson, who then informed the police. He and a PC Womersly had the unenviable task of gathering and transporting what was left of Mr Rider to the Queen Hotel.

The inquest was in Wakefield, at the Royal Hotel. All that could be returned by way of a verdict was 'found dead'. He was only identified because of his distinctive clothing, including a cap made of dog hair. Then his son identified the body. In these cases we search for explanations, but the best that the *Yorkshire Post* could offer was 'No reason could be assigned for him doing this…except that the old man has for some time past manifested symptoms of dotage.'

Cases: Murder and Accidents

Of course, there were plenty of murders during the period in which Mr Malcolm presided at the inquests. There was a serial killer, a 'Ripper', around Leeds at this time, and also several murders of 'ladies of the night', whose business made them particularly vulnerable. But, of course, at a coroner's court, in such cases, the important point was to establish that the death was not accidental, nor suicide, nor caused by such things as industrial accidents (also very common then).

Fortunately for the staff involved, there was usually no doubt – as in the instance of the killing of John Manley by John Ross in 1881. Ross was seen carrying out the murder, in York Street, by witnesses, but they were friends of the killer. However, nothing could have been plainer, because Ross had arrived at the the Railway Hotel in York Street, confronted Manley and said, openly, 'I have an old score to settle with you'. The killer then escaped, but he was well known to the police. At the inquest there was evidence from a whole range of people and nothing emerged that would have reduced the charge from murder to manslaughter.

Then, of course, there were the industrial fatalities, and these stories involve events that would make a modern Health and Safety inspector wince and rage. Typical of this is the tale of poor Emma Pudson, who was just 16 years old. She worked for Hinchcliffe's woollen mill on East Street as a sliver minder. The *Leeds Mercury* tells the awful events:

'About 12.30 on Saturday last she was engaged in partially cleaning three carders while the gearing was in motion, and while so occupied it would appear from the evidence, though no one actually saw the accident, that her dress was caught by the machinery, and she was thrown with violence to the floor…She did not survive many minutes…'

Through contemporary eyes, there are so many elements in that needless death that we feel a shiver of tragic sympathy and revulsion.

Malcolm and his Peers

Before Mr Malcolm there had been several other coroners, such as John Blackburn, who held that office when Victoria came to the throne in 1837. He was also a solicitor and lived in Blenheim Square. He did very well, and he also managed to hold down a number of other duties, such as company solicitor to the Reeth Mining Company. It was a lucrative business, and Mr Malcolm had several competitors when he applied. Everything concerned with coroners' duties and courts' functions was in the standard text *Jervis on Coroners,* and Jervis has much to say on how coroners were elected. The main qualifications were they had to be financially sound, they could not be aldermen or councillors, and they had to live within the electoral district. They also had to be unrelated to any specific party or to any source of patronage.

In John Cooper Malcolm, Leeds residents found the ideal man for the job. His four competitors were beaten off and one suspects that his sheer presence and air of authority gained him the position.

TWENTY

A Dangerous Woman to Know: Louie Calvert

'She was only the second woman sentenced at Leeds Assizes to suffer the death sentence.'
(David Goodman)

Lily Waterhouse was 40 years old in 1923, when Louie Calvert knocked on her door. Lily's husband had died a year before, and she had lived in Amberley Road for 14 years. She had no idea that Calvert had come to stay with her as part of a ruse to fool her husband Arty into thinking she was with her sister in Dewsbury, and that she was having a baby. Louie Calvert was indulging in one of her complex deceptions, as she was not only leading a life of deep ambiguity, but she was a person who enjoyed lying so that she could get the thrills of escape from her mundane life.

Louie had been a housekeeper for a Mr Frobisher the year before this, and he was found dead in the River Aire in July 1922. With hindsight it seems peculiar that the coroner did not ask more questions about this corpse. There was a wound on the back of his head and he had no boots on. At the inquest, little Louie appeared and stated that she had pawned the boots for a few shillings. All this was very strange, because Frobisher lived a mile or so away from where his body was found. Had he walked bare-foot to his death? Was it suicide? It is astounding that the verdict at his death was 'death by misadventure'.

That had been the first appearance of Louie Calvert in the records, and she was destined to be far more prominent than that. She moved on from Frobisher's place to marry Arty Calvert in Hunslet, and now she was away from home pretending to be pregnant. She had two children already: one living with Arty and herself, Kenneth, and a girl, Annie, who lived in Dewsbury. So here then was a strange situation: a woman of 33 turning up wanting a room, and then, unknown to the landlady, trying to work out how to get hold of a baby that she would pass off as her own. The obvious thing to do was to advertise, as you would for any goods. The advert in the Leeds paper did indeed work.

A teenager from Pontefract had given birth to a little girl in Leeds, and her mother saw Louie's advert. It did not take long to arrange the adoption, and all Louie had to do was lie low in her lodgings and wait until the baby was with her. In this phase of her life we see Louie Calvert the clever performer, acting a role in the community. The situation was extremely bizarre: here was a married woman living under an assumed name in another part of the city in which her husband had his real home, pretending to be there in order to care for her newborn, currently in hospital. Yet, strangely, that would have seemed a plausible tale; at the time many young babies were ill with all kinds of maladies, from diphtheria to scarlet fever. Clearly, many would be in hospital in intensive care, and the mother would visit.

Dangerous Deception

Louie's love of performance, of escaping from herself and going into a role, was changing. Formerly, when she worked for Frobisher, she wore Salvation Army clothes and acted the part wel, but, as if her life were a B-movie feature of the time, deception led to more problems in the Waterhouse home. This sprang from the fact that Louie was a compulsive thief, and her pawning of Frobisher's boots had been just one of many visits to the pawnbroker's with stolen items. Another startling aspect of Louie Calvert is that although she was very short and thin (in fact under five-feet tall) her personality was forceful and assertive. She was capable of instilling fear in people, using sheer egotistic control and toughness. So much was this evident to Mrs Waterhouse that she was at first frightened to say anything when she began to notice that various objects had disappeared from her home.

But she gathered some determination when she found pawn tickets clearly relating to the objects missing. This was a time, of course, when many working people were in dire straits, and habits such as pawning the best Sunday suit almost on a weekly basis was one desperate way of keeping a little cash in the house. Louie was reported to the police and went to court, answering the charges, but after that she returned to her lodgings, packed her bags and her baby and went home to Calvert's house in Railway Place, Hunslet. As earlier writers on the amazing diminutive Calvert have speculated, how on earth she managed to be so prominent and sociable around Leeds at the time she was supposed to be having a child in Dewsbury is baffling; she was a familiar sight to many, and, being distinctive in her build and speech, she would have been seen by people passing from one area of Leeds to another, perhaps commuting. After all, Hunslet was densely populated and many would have been around there who knew the family, so when they travelled into the centre they would have known her by sight, as she stood out in a crowd.

Murder

But before Louie Calvert was to leave to go home to her husband, she had some business to attend to in Amberley Road, and it was a deadly affair. It was all brutality and lies with her, and she was clever with it.

It was just before Easter when Louie left the Waterhouse home, and Lily had been seen going into her house one Wednesday night around that time, but, in those terraces, neighbours saw and heard a great deal, and there was very little privacy. People were sensitive to any unfamiliar sounds. Domestic arguments would be heard by several neighbours, for instance. On this occasion, a neighbour heard noises in the lodger's room and saw Louie as she left the house, carrying her baby. She told the neighbour that Lily was upset and that she (Louie) was going home. She explained the odd noises by saying that she and Lily had been moving a big bed.

At last Arty Calvert had his wife back, and also what he thought was his baby, little Dorothy. This was a happy time, of course, and they were up late. But the next morning Arty saw that there was some luggage in the hall that had not been there the night before. Unbelievably, Louie had returned to Amberley Road in the early hours and collected the large suitcase – at this stage in her career, Louie was clumsy. She was seen by several people, despite the early time of day, and these sightings would be valuable evidence later on. Even more surprising, she left a note. If she had not done that, then the chances are that the dual life she had constructed may well have kept her anonymous when the police started looking for the little woman who had lodged in Amberley Road.

They did indeed start looking for her, very soon after her dawn appearance, and this was because Lily Waterhouse had, of course, started a paper trail when she accused her tenant of theft. When Lily did not appear at an appointment, the police came to her house and there they found her body. She was lying on a floor in the bedroom; there was plenty of her blood evident, even to the extent that some blood had splashed on the wall. She had been battered on the head, as there was dried, clotted blood on her scalp.

The hallmark was there at the scene, though it was not perceived at the time: Lily Waterhouse was fully dressed – apart from her boots. There had been a violent struggle and the old lady had fought with some tenacity, as she was badly bruised, and it had taken several heavy blows to finish her. It is somewhat difficult to accept, bearing in mind the physical stature of Louie, that Lily Waterhouse had also been strangled. The killer, the police noticed, had cut up cloth to use to tie hands and feet, yet there must have been something else used to strangle the woman, as the ligature marks on her neck were wider than that caused by a strip of cloth. It is a gruesome thought that the noises heard by the neighbour were almost certainly the movements of the dying woman's limbs as she was shaking in her death-throes. Her murderous lodger, small though she was, had been binding her tight, in an effort to stop the noises made by her feet; neighbours would certainly have heard sounds and would have asked questions.

The Arrest

But then folk began to remember the woman with the baby, and there was also the matter of the letter Louie had left. It was the letter about the deceit over the birth supposedly in Dewsbury. As this was addressed to Mrs Louie Calvert, there was a lead there. She was soon to be tracked down, and this woman, who had enjoyed the strange thrills of moving from one name and identity to another for some time, escaping the reality she perhaps feared, opened her door one night in April 1925 to find DI Pass standing there. As has been said already, Louie was an unprepossessing sight and there was a terrible irony in the fact that one of her

Leeds Bridge, near where a victim was found.

assumed names had been that of Edith Thompson, the celebrated killer who had been hanged at Holloway in 1923.

The police work was very efficient; after Louie had covered up the questionable behaviour of going to the Waterhouse home with a response of nonchalance and surprise, saying 'Oh did she do herself in then?', the police went to work on the adoption and the Dewsbury connection. She was arrested and taken away, and at that point we have to speculate about poor Kenneth and Arty Calvert. The latter had just learned that the baby was not his, and he was now wondering why his wife was in the police station. Poor little Kenneth was now without his mother. At the Town Hall, Arty learned all the real facts for the first time, and while he was absorbing this, Louie was insisting that, when charged with murder, she didn't do it.

The Trial

The trial was in front of Mr Justice Wright. The court learned that for the two years before she moved in with Calvert she had lived hand to mouth, but had realised that there were ways of exploiting poverty and existing in various roles and guises to get by. Possibly one of the most interesting and informative of these was her time as a Salvation Army woman. But it is futile to seek for any deep religious feeling in this woman: the feeling generally is that they looked after her, and the organisation was easy to exploit. She went to Alpha Street Hall meetings, but it was all a front. Often small details speak volumes, and in this case it has to be noted that she had even stolen her bonnet from a *bone fide* Salvation Army member.

The author of the most exhaustive account of this case has mentioned a neighbour who knew Louie well, and she testified that the little woman had violent tempers and that she was capable of changing her mood rapidly and of using bad language. The witness said that the obscenities from Calvert were so extreme that she had banned her from coming into her home.

It is pathetically banal to report that when Louie Calvert was asked if she had anything to say before sentence was passed, she said simply 'Yes, Sir, I'm pregnant.' There is something very informative about that statement. It indicates a naïve facility she had for a child-like defence when cornered. Saying an infantile thing like that was tantamount to admitting that her sense of reality was very slender and her inner fantasy, feeding the outer criminal who was a predator in the streets of Leeds, was a truly frightening aspect of her.

Then something happened that had happened many times, perhaps most famously in the case of Mary Bateman (chapter four), and as she had constantly avoided any statements in the witness box with the argument that she was ill – and now supposedly pregnant – a medical inspection was essential. Dr Hoyland Smith went to examine her in a court cell, and, as with Bateman, a woman had to attend. She was from a jury of mothers selected for the purpose. But the difficulty was in keeping with Calvert's muddled and crazy career: there was no proof either way.

Sentence and Hanging

The result was that the death sentence was passed. A Leeds City Counsellor said at the time that he felt pity for her and added 'She was a little, thin-looking creature only weighing a few stones. I should never legislate on the lines of hanging a woman.' But others soon realised that there were two Louie Calverts: in the dock she had been quiet and restrained, but down in the cell she shouted abuse at her husband, trying to say that he was to blame. All he could say was 'It can't be helped lass.' But the woman who was seen by some as undersized and pathetic had done the awful deed, and of course had also been wily and cunning in the extreme. Her actions in court and before the magistrate when first charged show an amount of guile too. She dressed in black and to the local reporters she became 'the woman in black'. It has been said that she fussed over her appearance, as if she were still putting on clothes to be someone else – to project a persona which was not really her.

There was an appeal. In London she was again dressed all in black, and the context of the time was a difficult one with regard to hanging women; since the notorious Thompson case in 1923, the eight women given a death sentence had all been reprieved. It must have looked to many that this was going to be a case of yet another reprieve, as a petition had been signed by 3,000 people. Much was made in the press on the subject of her child – the question of what would happen to it and who might adopt it was something that sold papers. But the sentence was not quashed.

Louie Calvert was said to have gone to her death 'more bravely than many men'. One has to say that surely there was something manlike in her; as Shakespeare said of Lady Macbeth, 'Bring forth men children only'. There was an element in Louie Calvert that had a quality of the brutal, unfeeling detachment we see in serial killers, but very rarely in women, even of that category. Her reasons for killing were very different from, for instance, the example of Aileen Wuornos, the serial killer in Florida. In that comparison, it is Louie Calvert who is the enigma.

Louie Calvert was executed at Strangeways Prison in Manchester on 26 June 1926, sent to the next world by Thomas Pierrepoint. As the sentence was to be carried out in Manchester, the hangman would ordinarily have been William Willis, but it was arranged that Thomas Pierrepoint would do it, with Willis as assistant. The under-sheriff appointed hangmen, and he chose the Yorkshireman. Willis does not seem to have minded taking on the role of assistant, though. Steve Fielding has suggested that Willis was not entirely to be trusted, saying, in his biography of the Pierrepoints, 'Three days following Mrs Calvert's execution, he was again only employed as an assistant, this time to Robert Baxter, a man whom he claimed almost 10 years seniority on. His conduct was recorded as aggressive, irritable and full of self-importance. When he failed to secure the leg-strap on the condemned man satisfactorily tightly, he was dismissed.'

So Louie Calvert was lucky in one last thing – she had a competent man to see her smoothly and professionally into the next world.

TWENTY-ONE

Gone for a Burton

'The Burton factory was a town in itself.'
(Sam Bernstein)

The name Burton is still very much associated with clothing, and the clothes shops with that name are still there on the high streets of England. The hub of the Burton empire was always in Hudson Road, Leeds, between Burmantofts and Compton Road. This was at one time the largest clothing factory in the world, and Leeds people are brimming with memories of working there earlier in their careers, as so many local folk were employed there.

Montague Burton, who started it all, was born Meshe Osinsky on 15 August 1885. His origins were in the Jewish population of Lithuania. He first worked in a tailors in Sheffield and borrowed a sum of £100 to start his own shop, which opened in Chesterfield in 1900. When he made progress, he chose Leeds as the heart of the empire. Leeds was the textile centre of the land, of course. From the opening of the factory in Leeds, in which he first employed just 56 workers, his firm grew to huge proportions. The secret of his success was the belief that he should make good quality made-to-measure suits for men, and the saying was 'A five guinea suit for 55 shillings.' What he saw was that bad working conditions in clothing manufacture did not, in the end, bring cheaper garments to the buyer. He was convinced, when he started out, that more modern production

Montague Burton.

methods would revolutionise this. He clearly had something there, because his branches opened in Manchester, Sheffield and Leicester very soon after the first one flourished.

Hudson Road

Montague Burton Ltd. was formed in 1929, and he employed directly 10,000 men and women in very good working conditions. But there was also a total of around 100,000 working for the business indirectly, in subsidiary services. Burton always said that he paid the highest wages anywhere in Europe and that he had the best welfare provisions for his workers anywhere in the world.

The streets around the factory, stretching to Harehills and Burmantofts, surrounding St James's Hospital and up to York Road at the other side, were lined with red-brick terraces (some still to be seen today), and, in the heyday of Burtons, it must have seemed that this was indeed a world of its own, a network of home and work for so many thousands of Leeds families.

The men working for him in the first phase would begin in their teens as barrow boys and then later be apprenticed as cutters or tailors. But of course women machinists formed the bulk of the employees. The term 'welfare' stood for some important features, such as the fact that the works had the largest site canteen in the world and that he ran a health and pensions scheme.

From the Burton factory words and phrases came, notably the story that there was supposed to be an RAF office over a Burton's shop and there men would sit exams. But if anyone failed they were said to have 'Gone for Burton.' Legend also has it that 'The Full Monty' refers to being kitted out with clothes from the maestro, but that is debated. A memoir recorded by a former employee states that in 1959 'They used the phrase then for a full monty being a three-piece suit which they did for less than other tailors' three-pieces suits.'

Workers have recorded memories from working at the factory in the early days. One memory expresses the sheer size and scale of Hudson Road: 'If you were caught up in the crowds it was difficult to get through your garden gate, you could be swept past by the sheer volume of people.'

Other memories are generally very happy, such as this from a man now in the US: 'I grew up in Leeds...started pushing a trolley around the cutting room on 1 April 1964, and had 18 of the happiest years of my life in the Hudson Road factory.' Another positive recall is this: 'I had some lovely memories of learning to sew in the training room with Hazel and Carol. At their say-so, you were off to the factory floor. This was a nerve-wracking experience, you could not see to the other end of the factory, hundreds of sewing machines were humming away...'

Union Troubles

In 1936 there was an unauthorised strike, though, so things were not always rosy. There was a meeting of 6,000 striking workers in March of that year and the meeting lasted for hours. The fitters had put in a pay claim and it was not met, so things escalated. The workers were so determined that, as was reported then, they had lost over £60,000 in wages. After the meeting this statement was issued:

> 'Arising out of consultation with the general secretary of the union It is agreed: 1. That following a resumption of work the Leeds Committee Will at once review the fitters' claim which is the ostensible cause of The stoppage: immediately following the branch committee's review of The fitters' claim...the fitters shall be entitled to request the branch Committee to forward their case to the executive board...'

There had originally been 9,000 workers 'out', and, in response to the trouble, Bernard Burton made it clear that all but 200 in the finishing section would resume work in a week. He stressed that they would be welcomed back 'in a spirit of good will'. Two days earlier the union representatives had advised their members to return to work.

A Mr Conley, of the National Union of Tailors and Garment Workers, met workers at the Leeds Trades Hall and said that the union could do nothing and that a return to work was the wisest move. The only outstanding grievance was from the fitters.

In 1927 there had also been a strike – a very sudden one. A large number of tailors went out and the knock-on effect was that another 5,000 workers were affected. It was unofficial and done with speed and a sense of grievance; the problem came from a shortage of tailors, as workers from outside had been engaged in desperation to meet orders.

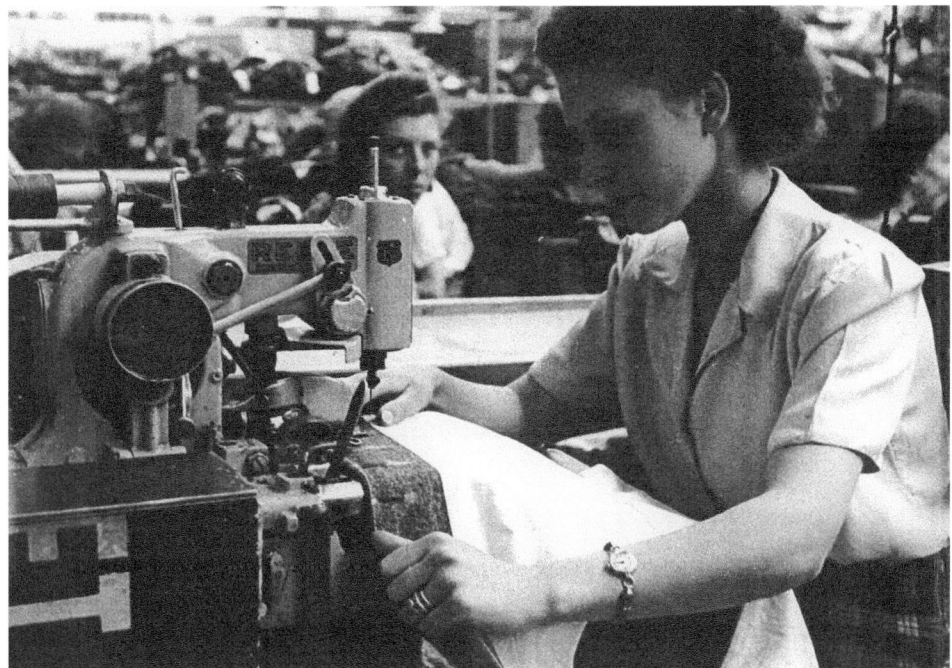
A Burton machinist.

Burtons said that the action was most unreasonable, as they had to meet orders in any way they could. Summonses were issued against the tailors, and their own union said that the only way they could be loyal was to remain at work.

On the really positive side, it has to be remembered that the Burton empire produced a quarter of all the uniforms needed by the British armed forces in World War Two.

Burton Summed Up

In 1936 Burtons gave £5,000 to the Council for German Jewry Fund. Burton always applied himself to the work for world peace and the improvement of industry; he supported the League of Nations and one of his regular contributions was a series of monthly luncheons in which men in power tackled issues relating to international relations, but also thousands of his workpeople attended lectures on similar themes.

In the end, these words from his obituary in *The Times* probably best sum up the achievement: 'In his business he introduced the highest standards of working conditions, health and welfare to promote good relations with his workpeople', but also that 'a great contribution was made to raising the standards of dress in this country'.

When Sir Montague Burton died in 1952 he had a chain of 600 shops and 14 factories. When he wasn't making money and running the business he was talking with university men, and it was said that 'he liked to have teachers and university lecturers around him'.

With their obvious concern for creating a pleasant working atmosphere for their employees, in spite of the huge size of the works, it must have been a deep sense of disappointment for the board and for Burton himself when they had the union troubles, but they weathered the storm and came through. Most memories from their workers are positive and complimentary. They seem happy that they 'went for a Burton'.

TWENTY-TWO

'Don't Ask the Price — Everything's a Penny' — Michael Marks

'But past the heaps of shirts and trousers
spread the stands of Modes for Night.'
(Philip Larkin)

As a recent article said, 'Michael Marks could not have envisioned in 1884 that bringing goods from town to country would see him crowned, 50 years later, as St Michael, patron saint of British knickers.' Marks began as a trader working the villages around Leeds, and then he settled for a market stall where his poster, proclaiming that customers need not ask the price, 'Everything's a penny', led to the 'penny bazaar' motto. He then formed a partnership with Tom Spencer, and, when Michael died in 1907, he left his son Simon to carry on the business.

Early Life
Marks was just one of a number of market men with big ideas, who flourished in the late Victorian and early Edwardian years; many were Jewish, like him, such as Jacob Cohen – who opened the first supermarket in Britain in 1958. It started in 1884 when Marks opened his Kirkgate stall, and then, in 1901, a warehouse was opened in Manchester in Derby

Street. The Leeds connection continued with the establishment of a branch store in the Cross Arcade in 1904; from that point on, Marks and Spencer were more than simply market traders.

Michael was born in Slonim, in Russia, in 1859, and he then emigrated to England in his teens. He could not speak English, but he was fortunate in that the firm of Barran (mentioned in chapter 17) employed refugee workers of a Jewish background. When he met Isaac Dewhurst in 1884 he found a man who had a warehouse, and so, with a base for produce, the deal was that Isaac would sell the goods to Michael, who would then go out and about in the suburbs and sell them on. There was no stopping Michael – he even opened stalls in Castleford and Wakefield.

Michael soon realised that as there was a large market area behind Kirkgate, and this could be exploited too, and that is where he began his penny stall – spreading the idea to other towns soon after. As the expansion continued and he needed a partner, Dewhurst refused, and so along came Spencer, who considered a £300 investment to be sound good sense. He had done his research well. That bought him a half-share.

The two men worked out the logistics, beginning with the sensible idea that Spencer would take care of administration and warehouse work, while Marks would stay where he was most suited – running the retail trade in the markets. Michael Marks had established a network of businessmen in the manufacturing side of things, and so he could build on these relationships and speed up progress.

In 1897 they had their Manchester warehouse and they also needed a distribution centre, because by that time there were 36 branches. It was a sign of great strides being made when the business became a limited company in 1903. Spencer had made huge profits by the early Edwardian years, as most of the main outlets were averaging £4,000 a year.

Landmarks

In 1908 the famous brand and early logo of St Michael were officially created and registered. Their penny bazaar idea caught on in London after they bought the company of that name. Then, in 1916, Simon Marks became chairman of the firm. By the 1930s the stores had cafés, and a food department was introduced in 1931.

In May 1933 Mr Simon Marks produced a report on the company and it was a totally satisfied, optimistic feeling all the way through the long text in *The Times*. He took a broad and reflective view of how Britain had changed and become a place where the department store was a keystone of cultural life. He stressed that 'free choice of our customers is the decisive factor'. Profits were certainly impressive then: in 1932 they had net profits of £670,117 and a general reserve account of £329,457.

The secret was, as Simon Marks explained, 'We help the manufacturer to reduce his costs in many ways – we enable him to make large purchases of raw material on favourable terms.'

Royal Shoppers

A landmark has to be the Queen's visit to their bazaar in 1932. That was a great honour, of course. She spent over half an hour there and bought an Axminster rug for five shillings and a tea service for six shillings. It was an age in which efforts were made by the media to make royalty more 'human' and to show their ordinary side, so reports stressed that the visit was not formal. Sir Simon walked with her and 'She constantly asked him about the origin of various articles, and expressed her pleasure at the great number which were of British manufacture.'

What she saw there that most interested her gives us a good insight as to what was on offer: mainly dolls, toys, blouses, jumpers (made in Lancashire she was told) and silk ribbons. Her Majesty was followed all the way around the store by a massive crowd of people, all amused and curious, as if the Queen never normally entered a shop – and, indeed, she rarely did. Marks and Spencer had brought her out to join them in everyday shopping and browsing.

The last role played by anyone in the Marks family was by Marcus Stieff, who retired in 1984. As I write this, the company have won back many of its customers after a successful advertising campaign involving stars such as Twiggy, after falling sales a few years ago. There is no doubt that Marks and Spencer will go on and on, remaining as a British institution. Michael Marks's barrow and stalls were destined for great things, and his name has become a Leeds byword for sheer bold enterprise.

It would be easy to justify the claim that Jewish people have had a massive impact on the retail structures and habits of generations in

Britain; these entrepreneurs have demonstrated the need for risk, innovation and planning in business success. Anthea Gerrie has pointed out in a recent issue of *The Jewish Chronicle* that Marks and his kind 'introduced mail order catalogues, cheap chic, designer boutiques and sex shops to the market-place before fainter hearts or less fecund imaginations considered them.'

Michael Marks is in that category, and so are the others of his family who followed him into this long adventure. As far as the Leeds context is concerned, I am old enough to recall long walks down North Street and I know that my pocket money regularly went to a stamp dealer called Mr Studley, who had a shop close to the now defunct Gaiety Kinema. There is still a Studley shop in Leeds centre. The Marks template is repeated a thousand times in Leeds, and it is there for all to watch and learn – a business spirit that made Leeds the new, stylish and vibrant city it now is.

Marks, the original founder, presented a pattern to so many locals; the rags to riches story did not have to be a wild dream: that was the lesson of his career. He had done what thousands of Jewish immigrants going to New York had done, for instance, and that was to go from barrow-boy to tycoon. One feels that he would have had more satisfaction from the fulfilment of that dream narrative of East European Jewry than from the sales figures, when it came to the maturity of his success, because he had achieved what very few in his position had.

The older Marks and Spencer's buildings also show a real sense of style. It has often been noticed and remarked on that what has always defined the firm is a sense of style and quality, somehow still overriding many of the claims of rivals even today and winning on those criteria, aspects of the company that are evident when we drop in the 'local M&S' on the high street.

TWENTY-THREE

Some Leeds Victoria Cross Heroes

'Pearson was wounded by a sword-cut to the right shoulder.'
(VC commendation)

The Victoria Cross is the highest military award for conspicuous gallantry, and it was created in 1856 during the period of the Crimean War. It was, from the beginning, open to all ranks. The cross has a crimson ribbon with the words 'For Valour' written on it. The very first crosses were made from Russian guns captured at the battle of Sebastopol.

A publication of 1893 describes the scene in Hyde Park when the Queen presented the first crosses:

'Sixty-two men of valour received the Victoria Cross from her Majesty in Hyde Park on the 26th of June. Multitudes flocked to see the interesting distribution. The Victoria Cross is a very plain affair, made out of the cannon captured at Sebastopol; a little leaden coloured Maltese cross with a red ribbon for the army and a blue ribbon for the navy. The decoration carries with it a pension of £10 per annum. The Queen, with that air of majesty and condescension so natural to her, pinned the cross on each brave breast...'

These are the stories of three of those remarkable men.

John Pearson

Several men from the Leeds area were to wear that cross. John Pearson, who enlisted in 1844 and joined the King's Royal Irish Hussars in Leeds, was originally a gardener, but he soon learned to use very different implements. His first large-scale military action was the Crimean War, and he embarked on that conflict in May 1854 on the transport ship *Wilson Kennedy*. He was in fact to join the famous Light Brigade, and he was in the second line when the charge at the guns was made. He was one of the lucky ones who survived, but his cross was not won there.

Pearson was to see action in another case of world significance – the Indian Mutiny of 1857. He sailed in June that year from Cork, on the *Great Britain*. His regiment was in action in Gwalior when the mutiny was finally ended, and the most remarkable part of that confrontation Pearson experienced was the death of the Rani of Jhansi. She was dressed as a *sowar* (a male officer) and on horseback when the British cavalry arrived. An eye witness describes the action in which Pearson won his honour: 'She attacked one of the 8th of their advance, was unhorsed and wounded. A short while later, as the British retired with the captured guns, she recognised her former assailant as she lay bleeding by the roadside and fired at him with her pistol. But he thought she was a man, and he 'dispatched the young lady with his carbine'.

Pearson was there at that time, and he recieved one of four VC's awarded to his regiment. A ballot decided who the four were to be. Pearson was one of the lucky ones – he had been in the main charge. Later, he was promoted to corporal and then sergeant (in 1865). He lasted almost the full stretch in his army career, pensioned with an annuity of £25 a year in 1867 after being invalided home. But he had also won the Meritorious Service medal. We know a lot about his career – more than many a VC winner: he was discharged unfit for service and then he settled in Halifax. He then emigrated to Canada and settled near Lion's Head, Ontario.

John Raynes

John Raynes, though born in Sheffield, died in Leeds and his body lies in Harehills Cemetery. He won his VC in France in 1915, and the reason can be found in *The London Gazette* on 18 November that year. He was in the A Battery, Royal Field Artillery, 71st Brigade. The citation notes that his battery was under heavy bombardment and the shells coming down on them were armour-piercing ones. There was a cry of cease fire, and Raynes went out to help the wounded. Sergeant Ayres was wounded and several hundred yards away from comparative safety when Raynes got to him and bandaged him. The casualty was then carried to a dug-out, and then Raynes went out again.

Later that day, having already been gassed because he gave his mask to a wounded man, Raynes was in a group of men who were buried in a house and cellar. Although he was wounded, he stayed behind to help the others. The citation concludes: 'Then, after having his wounds dressed, he reported himself immediately for duty with his battery, which was again heavily shelled.'

He had joined the army on 10 October 1904 and became a reserve bombardier, and so he was recalled to the colours when war broke out. When he came home he joined Leeds City Police and it comes as no surprise to learn that this astonishingly-able and brave man won promotion to sergeant. He retired from that profession in 1926, and he died in 1929 after being paralysed for three years. Just before he died, he received a telegram from other Yorkshire VC winners. He died two days after the Lord Mayor of Leeds, N.G. Morrison, had visited him.

Charles Ward

Charles was just 22 when he won his VC. He was a private in the 2nd Battalion King's Own Yorkshire Light Infantry, serving in the Anglo-Boer War. In May 1900 the 13th Battalion of the Imperial Yeomanry had been captured by Piet de Wet, the Boer leader, at Lindley. Only a month after that Lindley raid, there was desperate fighting and Ward's picquet from his regiment was blocked off from the security of the main force. There were Boers on three sides of them, and it was Private Ward who volunteered to carry a message for help. Death seemed certain, as he would be

Charles Ward VC.

going out into a volley of bullets, but he somehow managed to get through. Not only did he take the message, but he returned and was badly wounded in doing so. Without his bravery the picquet and their post would have been taken by the enemy.

He had crossed 150 yards of open ground, and so foolish was his request that at first his commanding officer had refused to allow him to go. We have to imagine that the young man persisted in spite of the odds being heavily against his surviving more than few seconds after showing his face outside the redoubt.

Ward was the last VC winner to be decorated by Queen Victoria herself; he became a Company Sergeant Major after that. Charles Ward is not buried in Leeds, his place of birth, but in Cardiff. The discovery of the now well-known films made by Mitchell and Kenyon contain an interview with Ward. This is now commercially available as *The Lost World of Mitchell and Kenyon.*

The Most Obscure

In reviewing the Leeds men who won VCs, one name is only very slightly known, and we know very little of the details, but his discipline and achievement deserves better recognition so I tell his brief story as a coda and to commemorate him with honour. His name was Edward McKenna, and he was a colour sergeant in the 65th Regiment. He took command of 35 men and charged a much larger group of Maori warriors. As the enemy scattered and night descended, he had to hold his men tightly in silence all through the hours of darkness. It could be argued that to maintain that situation was much harder than to have rashly charged or to have carried on firing – probably at shadows.

His commendation reads 'During an attempt to cross the Dialah River, Mesopotamia, he watched the two pontoons ahead of his raked by machine-gun fire When his own pontoon was hit and every man beside him had been killed, he tied a telephone wire to the pontoon, dived overboard and towed it to shore.' That was on the 7–8 March 1917. He also saved the life of a wounded officer.

Jack, born in Leeds, is actually buried in the Jewish Cemetery in Manchester.

TWENTY-FOUR

City Varieties People

'Ladies and gentleman your very own Mr Danny la Rue!'
(Leonard Sachs)

Leeds City Varieties, the entrance nestling off Briggate and easy to pass by, began as a 'singing room' as part of the White Swan public house, opening for business in June 1865. Thornton the arcades man owned it, but he sold it in 1876 by auction. It was leased to John Stansfield and then passed to his daughter. In 1894 the place acquired the name City Varieties, and it became known to millions well beyond Leeds when television cameras filmed the series *The Good Old Days* from there.

It is possible to trace the story back even further, because in 1760, when the White Swan was built, the 'singing room' clearly involved all kinds of 'turns' for a variety of customers. In 1908 the Ordnance Survey map shows the area it covered, and we know that there was a balcony and that it had a capacity of 2,000 people. There was even a snooker room somewhere within its walls.

In 1880 Stansfield put his name to the concern, letting it be known as Stansfield's Varieties. It became part of a larger outfit when Charles Morritt took

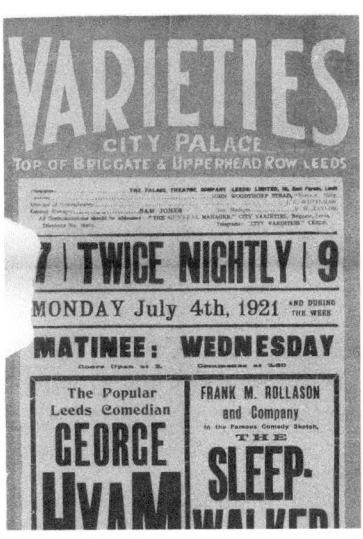

A City Varities poster.

over in 1880, as he owned other similar properties. But by that important date of 1894 it was known as the Leeds City Varieties Music Hall to the locals.

Development into the 20th century

In 1898 the Empire Theatre was constructed just along the road in Briggate and therefore the Varieties was sold. But the new owner wanted to maintain the music hall tradition, and it was re-opened in 1898, run by J.C. Whiteman. Music halls were booming in the 90s, and some of the personalities to tread the boards in Leeds in that decade were Charlie Chaplin, Lily Langtry the Jersey Belle and even Houdini, about to experience his failure with the Tetley challenge (see chapter 16). It was a time when there was a deep interest in regional identity and 'difference', and so dialect performers in songs, comic monologues and sketches were popular. An example was the 'Eight Lancashire Lads' – one of whom was Chaplin – and there was also the Lancashire comedian Morny Cash.

Fred Wood had been in charge, and he had also run the Queen's Theatre in Holbeck, but he died in 1913. The main opposition to the success of the business at that time was the coming of the silent films. Across the country, a number of music halls were in the middle of such hard times that they were demolished, but not the Varieties; it struggled on, though not perhaps with the usual class of stars performing. But it really was the age of variety, even to the extent of acts being 'novelty' – a term that covered a variety of sins as well as stars. Certainly that trend is exemplified by the work of Bryant and Bryant, billed as 'Australia's Novelty Manipulators'. They were the Edwardian equivalent of David Copperfield or similar today.

Of course, there was always another dimension to variety and that was entirely local. This was a tradition that carried on well into the 20th century, as in the 'turns' put on every week at Working Men's Clubs by local talent. In 1913 the Varieties gave locals a chance to entertain by holding amateur wrestling matches.

Stephen Griffin has described the acts in the great age of variety during the Edwardian years:

'Some of the variety acts were downright bizarre: along with the usual tumblers, acrobats, fire-eaters, jugglers, ventriloquists, dog-acts, contortionists and conjurers there was, for instance, a man who appeared on stage dressed in a voluminous coat, within which was contained virtually any train ticket or card that anyone could name; his whole act was based on audience members calling out the most obscure journey they could imagine...' (Stephen Griffin: *Ken Dodd: The Biography*).

The entrepreneur Harry Joseph took over in the middle of World War Two, leasing it from the White Swan Estate Company. It carried on regardless of the bombs and air-raid warnings. One story told is that a woman gave birth to a child in the audience on one occasion, and Harry Joseph is supposed to have given the child free admission to the theatre for life. From the Joseph era came Frankie Vaughan, real name Frankie Abelson (who was apparently a big hit with the Leeds University Rag review) and lots more, who today would probably be called C-List celebrities, although, on the other hand, the playbills tell the story of who was appearing there and some of them are still widely known or are part of nostalgia reproductions from the era of the music hall's golden days – performers such as Arthur Lucan (known to children everywhere at the Saturday Matinees as 'Old Mother Riley'), 'Monsewer Eddie Gray' and even, in 1957, Harry Corbett and Sooty. Many are now forgotten, such as 'Shogun and Rider – Sharpshooters' on the playbill in the 1930s.

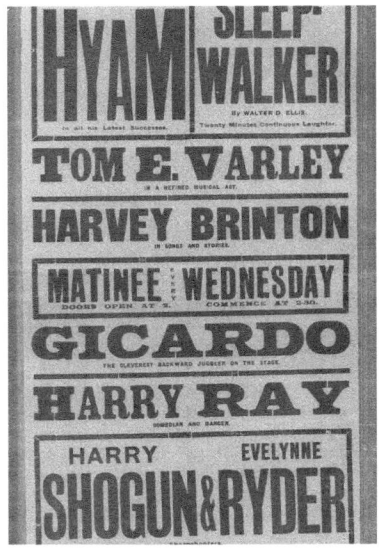

An old Varieties poster.

Arthur Lucan (Old Mother Riley).

'Monsewer' Eddie Gray.

However, many singers and performers were destined to make it in either the world of variety, theatre or operetta and their stories are often extraordinary, such as that of Lilian Neilson, of whom an early biography said:

Lilian Neilson.

'The story of Lilian Neilson's life is largely a story of hardship and sorrow. She was born out of wedlock, in or near Leeds, March 3 (probably) 1846. Her father's name is unknown, her mother, an actress, was Miss Brown...she was reared in humble circumstances and worked in a factory.'

But the theatre stories are often charming 'rags to riches' ones, and Neilson somehow 'Obtained a footing in the theatre and little by little she made her way to a position of some influence.' Her first big break was playing Juliet at Margate.

So many of the Varieties people had lives that would compare with that.

Good Old Days

In 1953 the theatre was used for a pilot programme on the old time music hall, and it was a big hit, considering that Joseph, not long before that, had been desperate to bring in the punters, and so had resorted to having striptease acts. This was still the time when the girls had to form a tableaux picture and not move any limbs. But such moves became outdated when, in 1953, *The Good Old Days* was broadcast and the varieties never looked back.

The show was devised by Leeds-based Barney Coleman, who had also produced the Wilfred Pickles programme *Have a Go*. In 1890 a three-pence entry fee entitled a customer to a glass of beer, a seat and a right to hurl abuse at performers who did not come up to scratch. By 1973, when celebrating years of the programme's success, it also held a long pantomime season of 19 weeks.

The City Varieties entrance.

The BBC took two days to record a show, having to remove some of the seats to install cameras in position. The stars rehearsed on a Sunday, the band were called on by the afternoon and then the whole show was recorded on the Sunday night, so the BBC men were packing up by Monday. The compère was Mr Leonard Sachs, known as the man who 'dined on dictionaries', and one of the traditional activities of the show was the crowd jeering at him as he spewed out strings of alliterative compliments about the performers. In 1973 there was a waiting list of 20,000 people to attend and don the Edwardian costume, only too keen to shout and heckle when required, and certainly to join in the hearty choruses.

Really Famous Names

Having noted that in its long history the Varieties had hundreds of forgotten performers, it has to be said that very famous people have also entertained there. One of the classic acts was that of the great Sir Harry Lauder, who appeared in Leeds in 1911. He was paid the sum of £11 and said to be 'rather good' Since then almost every well-known singer from cabaret and clubland has appeared there, along with the comics of the Ken Dodd variety.

The Varieties is without doubt a major Leeds institution, quite easy to pass and overlook, but the cultural historians will never let it be forgotten. It has recently been refurbished, after being sold to Leeds City Council in 1987, and it looks as though, if advertising is to be believed, *The Good Old Days* is making a comeback. Its position, still close to the inn-yard ambience of its origins, reminds us today that 'a good turn' is still something that can come from a real and genuine feeling of joy and relaxation, not necessarily from the smooth and professional practice of a craft – though both have had their place in this rich theatrical history in the heart of the city. There will always be a strong historical link between the early impresarios of the place and the spirit revived by the BBC in *The Good Old Days*.

TWENTY-FIVE

Murder by the Parish Church

'And the lonely of heart is withered away.'
(W.B. Yeats)

Mary Judge was well known around the area of Leeds along Kirkgate, between the Parish Church and the Regent Hotel. It consisted of a few streets and dark alleys, not far from the Calls – notoriously unsafe places for walks by night 40 years ago. But Mary, 40 years old and a cheery, sociable person, liked a drink and liked that area which in many ways a risky business, as may be seen even today, because there is an isolated patch of land (now a small well-maintained park) under the railway arches, and the trains above swing around on the viaduct before going on into the station a little further into the centre of the city.

Midnight Corpse

Mary was discovered just before midnight by a passer-by on 22 February 1968, battered and almost naked, with her clothes scattered around her body. She was only 5ft 5in, had brown hair, and she had been wearing quite garish clothes, definitely not colour co-ordinated, so that would have made her stand out. She was wearing a dark blue skirt with green shoes, a white blouse and a black check coat. She had severe head injuries.

The area was sealed off and arc lights set up in that dismal, shadowy patch of land. Superintendent Hoban of Leeds CID had barriers erected for the investigation and asked locals about her life to get a picture of

Kirkgate.

who she was and what could have happened to her. She was well known to the barmen of the pubs around the area, such as the Brougham, the Regent and other places up Kirkgate. People said she was 'always friendly and happy, liked a drink, and loved to stop and talk to children'. The patch of land is close to the Leeds central bus station, and at that time the area was notorious for its beggars and tramps. Tramps would often cadge money along the bus station platforms. By day it was busy: there was a huge Pilkington's Glass office nearby, and commuter crowds would walk from the buses, past the abattoir to Vicar Lane. By night, it has to be said, the area was well frequented by prostitutes too. Whether Mary was on the game is not clear, but one interesting point is that she lived in East End Park, on Glendale Street. This was a long walk for her, up towards the Shaftesbury cinema along the York Road. If she was a familiar figure down by the buses, she needed a good reason to walk more than a mile down to the pubs she liked – and alone.

The Investigation

But Mary's murder has a fascinating piece of drama to it: people saw her being attacked. This was because the Hull train rattled past the Parish

Leeds Parish Church.

Church at 10.18 that night, and several people saw the assailant. A small boy was the main witness. He came forward with his mother and gave a description of a tall man of slim build, with long dark hair and wearing a dark suit. Of course, this was February in Yorkshire, but the train passed within a mere 50 yards of the patch of grass where the killing happened. The 8.37 train from Hull would prove to be a key element in the investigation into the heartless slaughter.

Mary had also been seen outside the Regent Hotel in Kirkgate earlier that night, and it also became obvious that the killer would have had plenty of her blood on his clothes. Appeals were made to local dry-cleaners to be vigilant in inspecting clothes brought in for cleaning the day after the killing. Nothing came of that, so the train sightings became the main leads.

The Hull train was so important that a reconstruction was staged. Officers boarded a train at Cross Gates, and PC Eileen Playforth took the part of poor Mary Judge. It took just 15 seconds for the train to pass the scene; it was winter, late at night, and the grass was under the tall arches

The patch of land where the body was found.

of the high viaduct. But one positive thing emerged from this: a man was seen leaving the scene by a witness from Bradford, another passenger on that Hull train. At that point on the train's journey, and passing quite high over the patch of grass, the view would be quite distorted, but enough was seen by the man for him to make a helpful, descriptive statement.

Yet all this work and methodical investigation brought no positive result. Mary, a friendly woman who may have simply been lonely, and not looking for men-friends at all, was brutally killed. But whether she was in the area for financial reasons or simply to meet friends, there was a certain degree of risk in that place at that time.

Unsolved

Of course, readers of true crime stories like an unsolved crime: it opens up the possibility that the reader might come up with a theory. The Judge case is for sure a 'cold case' now, but everyone lives in hope of something turning up. After all, a murder that took place in Halifax in 1957 (again a woman on her own) was thought to be permanently unsolved until a few years ago, when Calderdale Police received a phone call referring to a man's deathbed confession.

But of all the unsolved murders in Leeds, this is one that reaches deeply into the atmosphere of the Leeds streets in the late 1960s. There was something in the air then, a sense of liberation and 'a good time' after the austerities of the decade before. People did socialise more around town, but some areas were a 'no go' and Mary Judge was an easy victim. Her openness to other people would make her very vulnerable. At one time some writers thought that she might have been a 'Ripper' victim, but that is now unsupported.

All we are left with is a Leeds mystery.

TWENTY-SIX

Brotherton and his Collection

*'When another Shakespeare first folio was put up for auction this year
it was sold to a London book dealer for £2.8m.'*
(James Reed)

In 2006 the Brotherton Library, Leeds University, put on a special display to commemorate an important Leeds event: the 150th anniversary of the birth of the man who gave a wonderful collection of books to the university. Some of the real treasures in that collection include a Shakespeare first folio (1623), Branwell Brontë manuscripts and a 15th-century *Book of Hours*. There is also the magnificent Parkinson Building – one of the great landmarks of the city, seen from across the landscape as one drives into Leeds from Wakefield.

Lord Brotherton

Brotherton was born in Manchester in 1856 but moved to Yorkshire in the 1870s, and it is there that he started one of the largest chemical works in Britain. But being a typically active and socially conscious man of his time, he also went into politics and was twice MP for Wakefield. He took delight in massing this stunning collection, which covers English poetry and drama of the 17th and 18th centuries, mediaeval manuscripts and Victorian literature and manuscripts. What he left was destined to be a unique collection for researchers into literary history and biography. He left around 750 books, but some have been sold over the years. The first base for what was to become this collection was at Roundhay Hall.

Brotherton was also at one time Lord Mayor of Leeds. He died in October 1930, not long after he had laid the foundation stone of the Brotherton Library, housed in the Parkinson Building.

In 1930 a newspaper report on the progress of the Parkinson Building noted:

The Parkinson Building.

> 'With the complete destruction of a block of houses, plans will be proceeded with for the construction of a magnificent library, for which, it will be remembered, Lord Brotherton has made the princely gift of £100,000.

After that will follow the ornate new entrance that will crown the whole design. The library promises to be one of the finest of its kind in the world.'

The Gems of the Collection

Without a doubt, the collection, which was donated to the university after Brotherton's death in 1930, contains some extremely valuable items. Brontë works always fetch amazingly high figures when auctioned, so the library's booklets of stories by Branwell Brontë, brother of the famous sisters, headed *Letters from an Englishman*, would fetch a massive sum if sold. The 15th-century *Book of Hours* is also outstandingly beautiful as well as valuable. These were books used for personal devotion: often they were given to wealthy men with the hope that the artist might receive some patronage from the recipient. The illustrations are always of special interest, as they depict life at the time and present scenes in great detail.

As for the Shakespeare first folio, around 1,200 copies of this collection of all Shakespeare's plays were printed between February 1622 and November 1623 and were sold for £1 each. Only some 230 survive. The famous Folger Library has 80, but Leeds has this one and it will surely stay there.

At the commemorative event in 2006, Chris Shepherd, the Head of Special Collections at the university, said 'These things are available for people to consult and use, but we wouldn't necessarily always have them out on display.'

Brotherton the Chemical Magnate

It is easy to overlook the fact that Brotherton made a great deal of money from things that have little association with the cultural life all these artefacts represent. He was an original member of the Society of Chemical Industry, and he began in that subject by attending classes given by Sir Henry Roscoe in Manchester. He established his first works in Wakefield, being helped by the Dysons of Middlesbrough. The firm made ammonia sulphate. He had tackled the challenge of producing pure ammonia from gas liquor; he sorted out that little problem and a pure solution of ammonia became one of his company's by-products.

In 1893 the Cassel Gold Extracting Company acquired the rights for a process he created for extracting ammonia as the source of nitrogen. By 1909 the company of Cassel he supplied was taking 10,000 tons of 25 percent ammonia liquid. Brotherton even devoted attention to the use of creosote and coal tar.

When he was presented with the Messel Medal in 1930, he made a point of mentioning how some of these had helped the colour industry. But in complete contrast, he also, during World War One, helped in the manufacture of high explosives. He then bought the Mersey Chemical Company, which had been using German-made colour products. All this is forgotten as the charitable and philanthropic works take the limelight.

Other Business

Brotherton also gave, in 1929, a large sum to Toc H in Yorkshire. This was £25,000 and it was given to the Prince's Endowment Fund. *The Times* described this charity in 1929: 'It has grown by the single-hearted fidelity of humble men who returned from the Ypres salient to face the no less heroic of the cause they loved in a huge industrial area stricken with a grave period of bad trade.' In fact, the man who started Toc H was Gilbert Talbot, a Leeds man, the son of a vicar of Leeds, Bishop Talbot.

Brotherton had been a liberal patron to the university before this, giving £20,000 in 1921 for the development of bacteriological research, applied to public health.

As to his other activities, in World War One Brotherton raised and equipped the Leeds Pals Battalion, the 15th Battalion, the West Yorkshire Regiment, and he also paid the cost of food for the men as well. He became a baronet in 1918 and a peer in 1929.

He died on 21 October 1930. People are probably not aware that his full name was Edward Allen Brotherton, and though he was born on April Fool's Day, there was nothing at all foolish about this remarkable man.

TWENTY-SEVEN

Revie's Support Team

*'We had a constant stream of footballers, especially
on a Monday morning.'*
(Liz Horsley)

To virtually every loiner the name of Don Revie does not need an explanation, but, for the sake of the record, let's just say that he was the football manager who made the Leeds team everyone with an interest in football knows about: the one with Billy Bremner, Jack Charlton, Allan Clarke and a host of others. That team made Elland Road rock – in every sense of the word. They won a stack of major honours on the field and ventured into European competition, where they impressed. My own memories of those heady days are most vividly represented by watching a 5–1 victory over Ferencvaros, and I recall watching Jack Charlton eat a pork pie with his pint in a Holbeck pub afterwards.

But what about the team in the limelight – the one that kept the men going, patched them up, gave them massages, took x-rays and so on? There was Les Cocker, who was a trainer-coach and coached the England team as well at one

Elland Road ground.

point, Bob English, the physiotherapist, and Syd Owen, the chief coach. In addition to that crew, there were the staff at St James's who did the radiography.

'The System'

The *Yorkshire Post* produced a special supplement at the height of the team's success, and journalist Terry Lofthouse asked what the secret of their success was. It was, he was certain, in the system of which Syd Owen and Revie were the centre. When Lofthouse wrote the piece, Leeds were contending for the top spot of the First Division, after being Second Division champions. The basis of the system was that someone would be out watching the team Leeds United played the following week: out there every Saturday looking closely at the next opposition.

Syd Owen – chief coach.

Syd Owen had the main part of that chore, and he wrote up a long report each time. He told Lofthouse it was 'Sometimes 1,600 words, on a complete analysis of each of the 22 players he had seen that day.' Owen explained that the opposition players were profiled in minute detail, as the journalist summarised 'Their strong points, their weaknesses, are all thoroughly outlined. Whether the player is a striking forward, a ball player or defender is all contained in the report. This is then filed away in the Elland Road archives for future reference.' It all seems so simple now – common practice for clubs in fact.

Harry Reynolds, the chairman at the time, explained that the result of the hard work was that Leeds had a 'wonderful spirit' and that was evident 'from the board down...'

As the team trained, Maurice Lindley, the chief scout, looked at potential future Leeds players around the land, and Bob English looked after the muscles and bones after each crushingly-physical confrontation. The 1960s style of play was very hard and demanded toughness in close physical contact.

When Leeds United were proclaimed champions in April 1969, what Don Revie told the *Daily Mirror* explains a great deal about his attitudes and why so much was achieved. After the goalless draw at Liverpool that clinched the title, he said 'I thought our defence was wonderful. We allowed Liverpool only two chances when they looked like scoring and that's some going. We would have liked to have attacked a bit more...' In other words, he enjoyed the moment, but was still critical and thinking of improvements. A leader like that needed a back-up team with incredible devotion to the cause.

Maurice Lindley was profiled in a special commemorative brochure, and it was noted there that 'He gained his wide experience with Everton.' He directed the club's scouting activities, and it was said then that 'He personally scours the British Isles for likely lads and has even been known on occasion to spend an evening at home.' What was written about Lindley could apply to any of the support staff: 'He absorbs work like a sponge.'

Syd Owen was captain of the Luton Town team that played at Wembley in 1960, and he was also Footballer of the Year that season; he was widely respected everywhere and everyone knew that he was talented when it came to passing on the experience he had gathered. When Syd was asked to say a little more about how he spent his time at Elland Road, he said 'Our job is to take the lads who join the club and prepare them for the first-team selection at the earliest possible moment. The lads must be prepared to dedicate themselves entirely to the game.' He also made the point that the Leeds stars were still 'working' for the club when they were off the field.

Les Cocker – Leeds United coach.

Les Cocker was training the England Under-23 team when, in 1967, he received a tribute from the club's press writers. They said what was valued was his quick and accurate assessment of injuries and 'the speedy application of the necessary remedial treatment'. But more than that, he had presence, respect and a first-class career record. Bob English, the physio, was known at the time for the way he devised a series of 'graduated training and development exercises'. And there was also Cyril Partridge, a man who looked after the junior team.

When it came to medicine applied to the team and their injuries over a recovery period, pictures of the rehabilitation room as it was in the mid-60s look very simple and plain through today's eyes. One photograph shows Bob English in the room, treating 'Sniffer' Clarke's foot. The only technical gear present appears to be large lights and traction equipment. There had to be lots of liniment around too!

Liz Horsley

The official leaflet explains that 'all players are examined on joining the club and are then subject to a complete medical check each season'. But what about the hands-on hospital work, when injured players were taken across the city to receive treatment? Who was waiting for them there? One person who was there and recalls the players arriving is Liz Horsley.

Liz was born near Leeds during World War Two, the daughter of a New Zealand-born father who came to England when he was two. Liz was the middle child of three, and she recalls that her father, a dentist, had a practice in suburban Leeds after doing very well academically at the Leeds Dental School. She has memories of living in different areas around the city and of going to Cookridge Street baths, ballet lessons at the Clock Cinema and taking part in ballet displays organised by her teacher Mrs Lilleyman, performed at the Empire Theatre. Liz is sure that the occasion of that display was an exciting time: she recalls that a ballerina from a 'big company' would sometimes visit the event. Her memories of growing up in Leeds in the 50s and 60s include shopping at Lewis's and Schofield's, and, as she says, 'window shopping at Marshall and Snelgrove's'. Her life also involved dances at the village hall, travelling on her scooter and being in the Girl Guides.

Liz then started her medical training at St James's, and she recalls that

Liz Horsley.

there was lots of friendly rivalry between Jimmies and the Leeds Infirmary. She is one of those people, like myself, who well remember travelling past the magnificent and unavoidable but now long gone Quarry Hill Flats on her way to Burmantofts. St James's was then the biggest hospital in Europe, but Liz brings to mind a friendly atmosphere and a good, rewarding place to work. She says 'We seemed to know loads of people in the hospital. Perhaps it was the nature of the work, especially if we worked in different areas of the hospital.'

The training she received meant that Liz would spend time in other hospitals as well, including the Dispensary (once in North Street, towards Sheepscar) and Killingbeck Hospital in Crossgates. The Dispensary, she says, was a 'dismal place' and she never liked being there.

It was when Liz went to work at a private radiology practice that she met a broader range of people. This was in Clarendon Road. The clients, she explains, were those 'who either chose to pay for their X-rays or were sent by their firms, insurance companies or employers for private examinations'. She has vivid memories of the sports teams who came. Leeds United were not the only clients: 'Leeds United Football Club in the glorious Don Revie days, Leeds Rugby Union, Yorkshire Cricket Club as well as some local celebrities and dignatories.' One event at the Elland Road ground she remembers was an Intercity Fairs Cup Final, for which she went along and took a very basic portable X-ray machine just in case of injury. Liz describes the meetings with the players:

'We had a constant stream of footballers – especially on Monday mornings following the weekend matches. Names that particularly spring to mind are Jack Charlton, Allan Clarke, Billy Bremner, Peter Lorimer, Norman Hunter and Gary Sprake. I remember also young and up-and-coming players at the time – such as Terry Yorath.'

Liz has a clear recall of a time when Jack Charlton came in after an important Wembley game, and she discovered that he had been playing the match with a broken toe. Football fans always suspected that Big Jack was made of iron. Then there was the occasion when Billy Bremner brought his son – this was nothing to do with football, but the boy thought he could fly like Batman and had done so from a bedroom window. Luckily, the damage done was limited to a broken arm.

Liz's clients were not restricted to footballers, as she treated Geoff Boycott as well. But although Liz has lived out of the city for a considerable time (she has not lived there since 1969), she still thinks of Leeds as her home town. She says that 'To walk through the restored arcades off Briggate or to walk through Kirkgate market always evokes vivid memories.'

Epilogue: the Fans

Leeds United fans have always had a bad press and many football people are always keen to bring to mind embarrassing occasions, such as the time Leeds fans destroyed rows of seating at Derby's ground. Of course there have been legendary rough-house rucks, but at the base of all this, from the 'scratching shed' to the Gelderd Road end, the massed Leeds fans possess, in my experience, the two most essential attributes of real football folk: philosophical acceptance and endless optimism. As far as Revie's years are concerned, I can recall men standing in the crowd and turning around to remonstrate with anyone using obscenities, usually with the words 'Watch your language pal…there's a lady present.' From what I know of Don Revie, he would have been exactly like that, as he was a true gentleman and a great manager: one who knew the right support network as well as how to pick a winning team.

TWENTY-EIGHT

In the Cricket Hall of Fame: Len Hutton

'I felt that I had a duty to be there on Monday morning to lend him my support.'
(Roy Hattersley)

In June 1958 *The Times* announced to the world that Len Hutton was out of test cricket: 'Len Hutton has informed the selection committee that for reasons of health he does not wish to take part in Test Match cricket this season.' P.B.H. May took over the captaincy. Hutton was almost 39 then, and there was a sinking feeling in the hearts of cricket fans. Hutton had never been robust; he had a light yet athletic frame and had had a few bouts of illness before. As the reporter added, 'The only benefactors from his present condition will be the bowlers whom he has played with such consummate ease for many years.'

Early Life and First Games
Leonard Hutton was born in Fulneck, Pudsey, on 23 June 1916. His father, Henry, was a builder, but cricket ran in his

HUTTON OUT OF TEST CRICKET

MAY TAKES OVER

From Our Cricket Correspondent

The following statement was made by Mr. G. O. Allen, chairman of the England selection committee, at Lord's yesterday:—

Len Hutton has informed the selection committee that for reasons of health he does not wish to take part in Test match cricket this season. The committee has accepted his decision with great regret and has invited him to serve on the selection committee as a co-opted member for the remainder of the series. P. B. H. May has accepted the captaincy for the remaining four Test matches.

This news will be received with widespread regret, not only in England, and everyone will hope that it does not mean the end of the Test match career of one of our greatest batsmen. Hutton, whose 39th birthday falls in a few days' time, has never been particularly strong physically. He is also a most conscientious cricketer, and responsibility of which he has had so much since the war, both as a player and a captain, rests heavily with him.

For the last two winters he has had much on his shoulders, when captaining his country means such a lot to him, shows how run down he must be feeling in a nervous as well as a physical sense. One can only hope that he will be able to build himself up for the visit of the Australians next year, and all will wish him a speedy recovery and many

Headline in *The Times*.

mother's side, as her uncle was Seth Milner, a good player back in the 1880s. Hutton had what he described as a 'strict but caring' upbringing, and much of that morality stemmed from a Moravian background, Fulneck having had a settlement of Moravians since the early 18th century. Len went to school at Littlemoor Council School in Pudsey, and it was soon noticed that he was a natural with a bat, joining his brothers to play in the first XI for the Pudsey St Lawrence Club. He was noticed by the great Herbert Sutcliffe, who said that he had seen 'a marvel – the discovery of a generation'. Following that, Sutcliffe made sure that young Hutton was taken to the Yorkshire Cricket Club, and he experienced the notorious 'winter shed' coaching there at Headingley. Hutton must have been inspired as well as awed when, in his teens, he saw Don Bradman score over 300 runs in a day.

Hutton was around several cricketing greats, as he spent time on the pitch and in the dressing room, but he learned quickly and in his apprenticeship he was given the chance to use his flair as well as the application of the fruits of hard discipline. But he was in the right place to learn: Yorkshire won the Championship five times in the seven years before the war with Hitler. Hutton managed 196 in one of his first innings for his county. He was totally dedicated to his county and to the team, saying at one point 'Had I been ordered to walk on broken glass, I would have instantly obeyed.'

England Opener and Main Career

Hutton was just 21 when he opened the batting for England in 1937, and in just his second Test Match he clocked up a century. It is generally agreed that some of his very best batting was seen against South Africa in 1939, but after that he went to serve his country in the war, in the Royal Artillery. It was in the army that something happened which was to have an adverse effect in many ways after: he damaged his wrist. It was a dislocation that happened in a gym accident. The damage was so extreme that he had to have skin grafts, and as a result, after prolonged treatment, one arm was more than two inches shorter than the other. It looked then as though his cricketing days were over. But from 1846 onwards he more than clawed his way back. As Geoffrey Boycott wrote, summing up the achievement, 'Leonard dominated the stage throughout his career, featuring in 79 Tests to score 6,971 runs for an average of 56.67. Richard (his son) in picking up five England caps, accumulated 219 runs for an average of 36.50, although he captured nine wickets at 28. For Yorkshire, Leonard made 24,807 runs.'

1951 was an important year for Hutton, as it was then that he became England's first professional captain and never lost a series. Year after year, and against the Australians, he led the batting and was so tenacious and resolute that the phrase 'Hutton's out, side's out' gained currency. In that period, though his health began to suffer, he was, amazingly, never captain of Yorkshire.

Hatterlsey's Tribute

One day in 1949 Roy Hattersley missed school to go to watch a cricket match. It was Yorkshire against Worcester, and Yorkshire were on the crest of a wave. They had lost seven wickets as young Roy went in, and Hutton was still batting. After he had eaten his sandwiches play resumed and Hutton was still in. Although Yorkshire lost, Roy wrote 'That was the day on which I decided that Leonard Hutton was the greatest man in the world.' He did not meet Hutton until 40 years after that game, but he wrote, for a newspaper, 'Even as I mumbled something about being a politician, not a cricketer, I realised that at least one of my boyhood ambitions had been fulfilled. Sir Leonard Hutton drove me to a match in his Rover.' Hutton also fulfilled the image of the gentleman cricketer that day as well, because after Roy asked if it were true that he had said he was as good as Bradman, Hutton replied 'I never said that...I wouldn't say a thing like that.'

Hattersley's tribute was best expressed in these words:

'He succeeded so comprehensively that he stood, without either helmet or armguard, to Ray Lindwall and Keith Miller. Then he led England to victory over Australia when we recaptured the Ashes. The story which those who played under him always tell concerns neither his cover drive nor his late cut...it is his reticence that they recall...'

Other Matters and Final Years

Hutton married Dorothy Dennis, daughter of a foreman of Lord Downe at Wykeham, in 1939. When he retired from cricket he became a director of a company called Fenners and he wrote on cricket for the *Observer*, together with three books on cricket. He also became an England selector and therefore something of a 'grand old man' of the game, and there is no certainty that he enjoyed that role. But any man who can be a cricket columnist for decades must enjoy theoretical discussion about the sport to a high degree, so perhaps he liked the high-level debate on players and strategies.

The Hutton that Hattersley met was the one who had become the expert guest speaker, humorous and calm. He was about to become president of Yorkshire CCC, but he died before taking up that post, on 6 September 1990. There was far more to the man than his scoring records. As someone once wrote, 'To admire Len Hutton merely for the quantity of his runs is like praising Milton for the length of *Paradise Lost*.'

Generations of schoolboys in Yorkshire have been imbued with that particular awe and respect for talented batsmen, and they are taught to admire flair and panache in addition to simply registering high scores or merely being adept at tactical defensive batsmanship. In Hutton they had the type that represented sheer lithe athleticism fused with a rare ability to *read* a bowler and practice that instinct for the right stroke at the right time. When the crowd came up with 'Hutton's out, side's out', they were

really elaborating on that feeling every cricketer knows, at any level, of just how important the confidence inspired by a key batsman is: a man who is hard to shift from that crease. Hutton was one of the very best of that type.

Hutton certainly inspired my father, and they met at some point, because the great man gave him his autograph. He was one of those regular images from the world of sport who impressed as he was, rather than having to be a 'celebrity'.

Len Hutton and his autograph.

TWENTY-NINE

Percy Scholes and the Love of Music

'Most novels are duller than Mr Scholes's reference book...'
(*Time* magazine)

It could be said that there are highly original artists, deeply creative people who have a natural gift for individual expression, and that there are enthusiasts who disseminate not only interest and vibrancy but a passion for something they are convinced is profoundly important. In the latter category was Percy Scholes, a Headingley man who did more than most to promote the cause of music whenever he could. He wanted to bring the pleasures of music to everyone, believing, with many others of his generation, that music was the supreme art, as Walter Pater said 'All art constantly aspires to the condition of music.' I feel Percy would have agreed with that.

Leeds Years

Percy was born in 1877 on 24 July in Headingley; he was the third child of Thomas Scholes, a commercial agent. What Percy came to represent was a type of person that proliferated in the late Victorian and Edwardian years – the autodidact, a self-taught man of letters or humanist. He was bronchitic all his life, and so his schooling was adversely affected by that. Instead, he read widely and at random, although music was always going to be his primary interest. To go from school to work was hardly what many parents would have wanted for their bookish son, because he started merely as an assistant in the Yorkshire College library. That was later to become the University of Leeds, and it was to be an ambience that suited his disposition. Percy was a lover of theory and history, and the writing behind and about music, and with that he began as a teacher, first of all giving lectures on music at Kent College in Canterbury and then abroad in South Africa. That was an extremely enterprising and unusual route to academic status, but such things were possible then before the era of the extreme specialist.

But after that beginning of rather random and vague association with adult education, his career began to take on a more orthodox hue when he gained some qualifications – the ARCM. That was achieved at the same time as he taught at an extension college in Manchester. In fact, as that course was what we now call 'musical appreciation', it explains much about what he wanted to do and where his aims lay.

This more structured academic life was confirmed when he qualified for his B.Mus. in 1908 at St Edmund Hall, Oxford. He found time to marry in 1908 but was also busy doing something truly innovative: he conceived the notion of home study. This had been developed during his time teaching adults in the Co-operative Holidays Association, and it was a step in education that found a ready response. The result was an organisation called the Home Study Union.

Journalism and Teaching

Percy Scholes became the key figure in the home study field, and he edited the journal *The Music Student* for many years; he also ventured into music writing for the papers, becoming the music critic of *The Evening Standard* for seven years and also writing for *The Queen Magazine*. It was not an easy time for him: newly married and with no regular salary, he was existing essentially as a freelance,

Percy Scholes.

but, as long as he was prepared to travel around, he had work, because Oxford, Cambridge and London all wanted his services for lecturing.

He learned by hard experience and could turn his hand to anything within musical studies; he was busy during World War One and made sure that his expertise was employed in a scheme for the YMCA with the soldiers as the audience – this was 'Music for the Troops'. It was inevitable that he would progress in his writing from articles and lesson notes to books, and a man with his wide knowledge was ideal as a writer of reference works, so his book came in 1919, *A Listener's Guide to Music*. He later wrote the *Oxford Companion to Music* (1938) and other books.

What really brought his popularising talents out was his involvement with the media beyond print. Although he became a music critic for *The Observer* in the 1920s, he also found that in broadcasting he could really reach people and educate them in musical knowledge. The natural slot for him was in a weekly talk, printed as well as broadcast, and the *Radio Times* was the perfect organ for this type of dissemination of knowledge.

Quite a Public Figure

His versatility also brought Percy some involvement in business and in actually earning some decent money: he wrote annotations for the pianola rolls when that instrument became popular. It could be said that when he had a little more financial security he 'went global', as his ambitions for the state of the brotherhood of musicians and musicologists were that there should be greater communication. As he had moved to live in Switzerland he began international conferences, and of course that led to the inevitable lecture tours: he was a natural networker, industrious and tireless it must have seemed, usually working on several projects at once.

Even Sir Charles Grove, the doyen of musical encyclopaedists, was in awe of Percy's reference works, and it was well known that Percy Scholes was the man for a discussion or a round table when there was a music subject in the news.

During World War Two he moved around a good deal, and he was fond of moving his base: sometimes he was in Wales (where Aberystwyth was a welcoming musical fraternity of scholars and composers) and at other times in Oxford. He still moved around a lot even after the war but found time to write more books including the *Life of Dr Charles Burney*, the friend of Dr Johnson and the first major musical historian in England.

The Man

At his death in 1958, when the bronchitis had finally weakened him so much that he could not recover his health, *Time* magazine wrote of him:

> 'Died. Percy Alfred Scholes, 81, British music critic and historian, witty, unorthodox, occasionally prissy lexicographer, who wrote the entire 1,195 page *Oxford Companion to Music* in Switzerland. Most novels are duller than Dr Scholes's reference book, in which harmony is "the clothing of melody" and form is "one of the composer's chief means of averting the boredom of the audience".'

Awards came his way in abundance, including the OBE in 1957, a D.Litt in 1950 and another D.Litt from his native Leeds in 1953. The National Library of Canada now has his huge and valuable library.

But we also know the man through his friendships and how he relates to others, and the friendship with John Owen Ward has been documented well. Ward wrote to introduce himself to Percy, and he was to find endless help and fatherly advice from that moment on. Much of their correspondence survives. Ward told Percy that he had 'left school in 1957 with the Higher Certificate' and that his chief studies had been in the violincello. He was six years in the army and was a gifted linguist. By 1949 he was in need of making something of himself and Percy helped. The two men worked together and Ward became the obvious choice to take over the editorship of the *Oxford Companion* as Percy got older.

The advice from master to student would be handy for anyone, 'Write…(a) interestingly (b) clearly and (c) precisely. Make yourself a list some time of what you think are the qualities of the book that have made it the bestseller it is. Can you at present reproduce those qualities?'

There was always Leeds in Percy Scholes. John Owen Ward wrote the obituary for the *Dictionary of National Biography*: 'Traces of his native Yorkshire speech remained with him to the end.' Ward also said of his friend that one of his wishes was that 'the common people heard him gladly'.

THIRTY

Poet Laureates? Austin and Harrison

'These poems about you, dad, should makes good reads
For the bus you took from Beeston into town
For people with no time like you in Leeds.'
(Tony Harrison)

It would be a hard task to find two poets as dissimilar as Alfred Austin and Tony Harrison. The former was a middle-of-the-road Victorian who liked to retreat from the world and write letters to *The Times*. He was Poet Laureate and believed in the Empire and the Crown. Tony Harrison made it clear in an interview that the Laureateship was 'ridiculous', and that he was 'a great republican'. His poems have always tackled subjects of urgency, politicised commentary on people and ideas. He has been 'in the thick of it' and one feels sure that he has no time to write letters to newspapers.

Yet they have one thing in common: they were both born in Leeds. That city has been home to hundreds of writers, not all famous or influential, but nevertheless there is something about life there that has always pushed residents to express reflections, maybe due to the obvious divisions, oppositions and differences there. When I was a young writer, going to evening classes at Park Lane College and reading classic writers for the first time, I used to walk away from the evening class acutely aware of the stances that writers tend to take up. They love and they hate in equal measure and the hatred is coloured with disappointment. In my case that came from a profound attachment to the city of my birth. It is interesting that the other notable difference between Austin and Harrison is that the former left Leeds, both as a source of imagination and as a place to live. Tony Harrison has written about Beeston, and done so from all kinds of angles.

Alfred Austin

Austin was born in Headingley on 30 May 1835. His father was a merchant and his mother the sister of the MP for Honiton, Joseph Locke (a well-known railway engineer). Austin had a sound education, going to Stonyhurst and then the University of London. After graduating, he aimed at a career in the law and spent some years in preparation for that career, yet he never took it up. Instead, he tried to find success as a writer; it took some time to make any progress, but, with his satire *The Season*, he was noticed in some places where it would do him good. His tragedy, *Savonarola*, was published in 1882 and then several collections to the end of the century. Everything in his work comes from that tradition of nature poetry most of us know through the great Romantics such as Wordsworth and Keats. Much of his position with regard to how he saw poetry can be seen in a letter he wrote to *The Times* in 1910, headed 'Poets and the Simple Country Life.' In this he writes, in response to a statement that Wordsworth was the only true nature poet:

'And how about Shakespeare and his "wood notes wild"? Surely in what you wrote on Wednesday, you must have been thinking of London as it is now. In Shakespeare's time it was a village capital in the heart of the country, from which you could sally afoot into lanes and streams in a few minutes...'

Austin also made it clear that he was allied to that view, and he commented 'I have sometimes thought that the pessimistic tenour of certain writers in verse in our own time...sprang from their living for the most part in towns..'

He became Poet Laureate in 1896 and he took on the role with a purpose,

Alfred Austin.

wanting to express his views whenever he could. But the familiar problem with Laureate poetry is there with him for sure: he wrote in response to all kinds of events and the results were uneven. This brings up the old debate on the virtues or otherwise of 'writing to order'.

It says a great deal about Austin that his most popular poem was called *The Garden that I Love.*

Austin was at Oscott as part of his education, and that was the college which was influenced by Cardinal Newman (Austin's father was a Catholic); Austin was very much affected by the friendship of Newman, and in Austin's autobiography he reprints letters written to him by Newman.

Somehow, Austin found patronage and support in his writing all the way through his career, even having his first poems published (when he was 19) and paid for by his uncle, *Randolph, A Tale of Polish Grief,* yet only 17 copies were sold. He was not, however, discouraged.

He travelled much in Italy and then came back to England in 1864. He did try to get involved in other things aside from poetry – he stood as a candidate for Taunton (Conservative of course) but was bottom in the list. He married Hester Mulock and, of course, he needed an income – not something usually associated with the writing of poems. He found a job with the *Standard,* became a more keen Conservative and received encouragement from Disraeli. It would be wrong to assume that he failed at that and retreated into rural verse. He actually did produce some work in relation to political events, such as the 1878 Congress of Berlin; there he would have spoken to and more likely listened to the great Iron Chancellor, Bismarck.

A memoir written about Austin in 1913 is dismissive of his work, though expressed with a touch of irony: 'As a poet it would be untrue to say that Austin ever ranked high in the opinion of skilled judges. Though his verse was fairly popular with the general public.' A back-handed compliment if ever there was one.

A Laureateship with no Fuss

It is clear from the choice of Laureate after Tennyson's death in 1890 that there was something of a flat, bland feeling about the whole issue. The memoirist writing in 1913 commented that there were three informal claimants and that these all wrote to the Prime Minister to apply. Along with Austin were the Welsh poet Lewis Morris and Sir Edwin Arnold. 'Lord Salisbury was perplexed and kept the post open for four years', writes the anonymous commentator. But finally, at the very end of 1895, Austin received the letter to say that the Queen approved of his appointment.

It is reasonable to say that he did not impress very much really. Writers with opinions on that at the time tended to think that he did the duties 'quite well', and so they damned him with faint praise. He liked to write patriotic verse, of course, and so 1905, the centenary of Trafalgar, was perfect for him to write at length and with rhetoric on the theme of British victory. But some of his views were so conservative and conventionally blinkered that he could be crass, as in his opinion of the Suffragettes: 'He wanted the ladies who had no vote to desist from causing "pother"' because, 'Of all human relations, that between the sexes is the most important and the most operative; for on it repose the happiness of the hearth, the decency of society and the stability of the state.'

Austin did sometimes emerge from his rural retreat to lecture and make public appearances, and he also wrote dramas best described as 'closet theatre'. Austin died in Ashford, Kent, on 2 June 1913.

Tony Harrison

In 1987 Channel Four broadcast something called a 'film poem'. It was called *V* and it presented a dramatic and filmic narrative of Leeds United football fans, a cemetery in Beeston and a dialogue with the past and present, strongly political in the widest sense and with Harrison himself intercut, reading his work to a large and attentive audience. This was arguably the time at which England began to notice the Leeds poet, who put Beeston on the map.

Tony Harrison, born in Leeds in 1937, was educated at Leeds Grammar School and

Tony Harrison.

The graveyard at Beeston.

at Leeds University. From the start he was immersed in the love of language, both how it works to express belonging and how it can divide communities. He became a literary fellow for Northern Arts twice in the 1970s and then was resident dramatist at the National Theatre in 1977–78. His first poetry collection was *The Loiners* and there, of course, his Leeds roots were explored, along with much wider themes.

Harrison has also adapted classical works for the theatre and written translations; his films include *The Shadow of Hiroshima* in 1995 and *Prometheus* (filmed at Ferrybridge) in 1998. He now lives in Newcastle-upon-Tyne.

He has made a statement about his art and the central view here is this: 'I believe that maybe poetry, the word at its most eloquent, is one medium which could concentrate our attention on our worst experiences without leaving us with the feeling, as other media can, that life in this century has had its affirmative spirit burned out.'

The Leeds in the Poetry

Cover for the collection, Permanently Bard.

In an interview with John Tusa, Harrison explained that his work is a quest for 'public poetry', and it becomes clear that he has always wanted to make poetry part of experience, as everyday as most other things but with its own place and space. In that interview, he explained that members of his family were a great source of 'material' for the early poetry, such as his uncles. It went like this:

Tusa: 'You also had two uncles; one who stammered and one who was dumb.'

T.H: 'One was deaf and dumb and one was…had the most terrible stammer I think I ever encountered.'

Tusa: 'What effect do you think that had on you and your wish to be as articulate as you could be?'

T.H: 'These things only become clear in retrospect. I was aware of a hunger for articulation, it came not only from the fact that I had an uncle who was deaf and dumb and one who stammered but a father who was reticent, shy, unable to express himself…'

In common with so many other creative artists of all kinds, Harrison drew from his family and immediate locality a way to make images and to speak of difficult, complex things. Beeston gave him that. For instance, he says of his film *Prometheus* that it was 'taking an ancient dramatic theme and dropping it into the Yorkshire of my boyhood and seeing…seeing how the two get on…'

His Leeds identity was, of course, most easily evident in his speech, and a poet from a regional context is always faced with the need to be a part of that interplay between the literary and standard language and his own words, as in his roots. Harrison deals with this in his poem, where he writes of 'Them and us' with the phonetic representation of the Leeds version 'us' and 'uz', which proves to be an excellent way to write about that gap between instinctive language and the formality that writers always face.

V – Book and Film Poem

It was in his narrative of Leeds United fans and the oppositions in society that we perhaps see most engagement with Harrison's family and sense of place in Beeston. The poem has a profoundly drawn landscape covering that long slope from Beeston Hill, extending to Elland Road and also towards Churwell at the end of Beeston. The poem puts that Leeds landscape firmly in place as he locates his family 'blood feeling' in the tensions and divisions of the graveyard graffiti.

Anyone growing up in Leeds in the 1960s in particular could hardly miss the social problems associated with football gangs: the allegiance to teams in Yorkshire is always strong and sometimes aggressive. A Huddersfield-Barnsley game or, in earlier times, a Leeds-Bradford game would guarantee some enmity, and not always friendly. But the Leeds context of this poem/story is writing that tackles the deep resentments of the poor or the deprived. The divisions of wealth, language, attitudes, history and self-identity are all in the warp and woof of this stunningly-powerful book.

Laureates?

Austin revelled in his role of Laureate: he took every chance to promote the institution and he loved the public roles attached to it. Harrison has no time for it. There was therefore considerable interest in the topic when Ted Hughes died. Harrison was in the discussions in the press when journalists played and speculated with the potential successors. But somehow it seems entirely fitting that the Leeds man stayed out of it. His ma once commented that he wrote 'Mucky books' and that surely would not be appropriate for a Laureate. Alfred of Headingley would turn in his grave.

THIRTY-ONE

Queen of the All Girls' Band

'Five hundred girls passed under her baton.'
(*The Times*)

In the age of swing, as well as in the pop world, girl bands go back much further than many may think, and in some ways the first of them all was Ivy Benson's combo. Ivy broke into the male-centred world of the 1930s dance bands – an achievement enough to rank her with the heroes of this book, if she had not done anything more. But she did far more than that, and Ivy and her succession of all-girl bands were a feature of light entertainment for decades.

Early Life

Ivy was born in 1913 and there was music in her blood. Her father had been a pit-player at the Leeds Empire, and with that pedigree it comes as no surprise that she was fixed up with piano lessons as a toddler. At the age of just nine she won a talent contest and her career was off on the right foot. In addition to the piano, she learned the saxophone and the trombone. In the 1930s those two instruments were enough to open up an endless succession of arrangements, in an age where arranging was at the core of light music and, of course, radio arrived and made even more entertainment formats available.

But it was not music all the way for Ivy; she started work at Montague Burton's and played part time when she had the chance. There were girl bands around, and she played with one who had the dazzling name of

Edna Croudfoot's Rhythm Girls. Ivy mastered the clarinet as well, and she was equipped to be a formidable force. What was just as important was that she always had drive and no shyness problems. When it came to breaking into the world of professional musicians, organisations such as Mecca were the natural first openings and she was fortunate in having Jack Hylton as an admirer; he thought she was worth encouraging and he won her a spot on the radio in 1943. As the saying goes, after that there was no looking back.

Radio Days and The Ballroom

It is a record of shameful moves on the part of some of the people on the music scene when she made that opening, because ruses and schemes were done to try to ruin her and her band – the rival bandleaders clearly saw her as a threat as she was more than just a novelty. The shame comes with the addition that wrong notes were secretly placed in the scores of her band, and so aggressive did the campaign against her become that the bandleaders protested to the BBC by sending a petition.

With hindsight, the explanation is simple – they were jealous. Ivy Benson's All Girl Band was a marvellous success, with a large fan base and plenty of bookings. Ivy and the girls had played almost anywhere before the big break: the 1930s was an age of tea shops and dances at the palais, and she did them all. Of course, the war had the effect of reducing the numbers of the male opposition, and so her chance came and she took it. Her band was a 20 piece one, so they could be adaptable and tackle all kinds of popular music genres from jazz to swing. When the Mecca ballroom company really wanted her as a regular, fame had arrived. What really endorsed her arrival among the big stars was a 22-week spell at the London Palladium. Glenn Miller's impact in particular had made swing incredibly popular, and all that was needed was a variant on the visual pleasure of the entertainment – as long as the quality of the music was high. Ivy and her girls had both those elements.

Of course, it was not an easy job to recruit women musicians at that time. There was no long line of unemployed women players, so she had to find likely candidates and then coach them. There were places to look, and being a Yorkshire lass she knew about brass bands; there was female musical talent in those ranks so she went scouting. The same thing applied with the musicians in the then-vibrant Salvation Army bands. The main challenge when the recruiting was done was to take these players from their traditional modes into the swing and jazz era.

On the other hand, she lost girls as well – mainly through marriage and other relationship-related events of course. The GI bride trend was one factor. Her girls were naturally very attractive and so there were rival claims to that of musical fame. But when success came it meant that the name Ivy Benson was spoken in the same conversation as references to names such as Geraldo and Jack Payne. The celebrity status was universally confirmed when the band played at the 1948 Olympic Games, and it is remarkable that Lord Montgomery, hero of El Alamein, requested that she play in the victory celebrations when the war was over. Ivy Benson was becoming familiar to almost everyone and it was nothing to do with 'novelty value' – the talent ran deep through her bands.

Rise and Decline

The triumphs were so many and the bands lasted for so long that it is difficult to select what was the peak of Ivy's career. But in their heyday they were often on television and at the Palladium. The Isle of Man was their patch in the summer seasons. It was not really until other media came along in the 1960s, with the massive revolution in the nature of pop and rock, that the signs of decline appeared. Stepping down a few leagues, like a top football team that had suffered relegation, was inevitable, which meant performing at such places as civic dances and even at Masonic halls.

Ivy retired in the early 1980s, but the chronicles of her long career show that she never lost the itch to entertain and she was still playing locally even then, delivering her signature tune 'Lady be Good' at Clacton, her retirement place.

At the height of her popularity the reviews were generally favourable and enthusiastic, but there was often a tinge of sneering or damning with faint praise directed at amateurs, and Ivy was good enough to play at some of these, as in this review from 1956 headed 'The Lady Ratlings on Parade: Taking his present cue, Mr Jack Hylton now presents them – with Miss Ivy Benson and her band in the orchestra pit – as an all-feminine variety show.' The Lady Ratlings were wives and relatives of members of a charity organisation. Ivy did her best to raise the level and the mean-spirited reviewer won no sympathy.

She must have thought back fondly on the good times, and there are anecdotes that typify the kind of life she and her band led, such as the incident at Checkpoint Charlie in Berlin, when they had to get past some Russian border guards who were not co-operating. Apparently, the band played especially for the guards – *Il Silencio* was the tune and it did the trick.

The Subject of a Play and a Robbery

ADELPHI THEATRE

" THE LADY RATLINGS ON PARADE "

The end of term is already in sight, and here are some theatrical parents doing a little breaking-up of their own for three weeks before the children return. The Lady Ratlings are the wives of members of the variety artists charitable association, the Water Rats. Like their husbands they perform from time to time for charity, and recently they have, apparently, had some success on television.

Taking this as his cue, Mr. Jack Hylton now presents them—with Miss Ivy Benson and her band in the orchestra pit—as an all feminine variety show. As one exuberant, well-meaning but not particularly talented performer follows the other, an ungallant male might be inclined to recall under his breath that phrase of M. Montherlant's: " *Pitié pour les femmes !* " but the exclamation would be ill-judged, for the show bucks up somewhat towards the end of the second half with the appearance of one or two artists of real professional accomplishment.

Review of 'The Lady Ratlings on Parade'.

In 1984 Ivy became a fictional character as her band and their lives attracted the attention of playwright Liane Aukin. The Birmingham Rep put on *Silver Lady*, and the review in one paper sums up what the angle on her was:

'Ivy Benson, who rose from a poor childhood in Leeds and years as an exploited clarinettist, leading Ivy Benson's All-Ladies orchestra all over the world in the 1940s and 1950s, deserves a niche in some kind of pantheon. She was artist, teacher, general and Saint Joan; but judging from Liane Aukin's play, she is a treacherous dramatic subject.'

The reviewer's problem was that Ivy had been shown in a way that mixed the feminist elements with the 'rags to riches clichés'. But regardless of that, it was an enormously important event – a tribute few like her ever had. The play certainly brings to life the girls in her units: 'The girls develop independent characters – Tara Soppet as the boyish blonde taking to drink over 20 years...'

In 1977 Ivy's home in Chiswick was robbed by two men. They stole jewellery and a mink coat worth £3,000, and they ended up with a jail sentence at the Old Bailey. But the worst thing about that terrible event was that Ivy's aged father, Douglas, was assaulted. He was hit with a piece of tubing and tied up. The two unemployed men pleaded guilty and went to prison for three years. That was all a part of the price of fame.

Ivy Benson died on 6 May 1993. She had been a forces' favourite, a regular on radio and television and an undoubted impresario as well, employing over 500 girls in her bands. It would not present a difficult argument to insist that she should be in the modern pantheon of feminist icons. In her obituary, the phrase 'the doyenne of the dance-band circuit' does her justice, and she has to rank with the very best Leeds artistes of those wonderful dance band years and beyond.

THIRTY-TWO

Villains Unknown, 1948

'It was an attack from nowhere, by person or persons unknown...'
(Local reporter)

Ann Barker Murder

Ling Lane, Scarcroft, was a very quiet place in 1948, and it still is, by contemporary standards. Ann Barker lived in a cottage on the lane, in the middle of a beautiful part of north Leeds, not far north of the ring road at Seacroft. There is nothing left of the cottage today, though the place where these things happened is still part of a long line of attractive homes. But the new year was to start tragically in Ling Lane.

An idyllic place – but she kept a shotgun

As was the practice then in rural areas, Ann Barker kept a shotgun, and in her case it was rammed into a roofing area. But just after Christmas in that fateful year, a visitor came into her house and battered her to death. No one had touched her gun.

Neighbours found her body lying on the floor near the door, and it is some indication of the closeness of the community at the time when friends came to see why Ann's routine had not been kept: the most visible sign being that her newspaper had not been taken in. She lived a quiet life; she did some cleaning for a wealthy neighbour and had kept herself to herself, particularly after the death of her mother in 1945.

Scarcroft is an idyllic place, but the peace was disturbed once the investigations took off. West Riding detectives got to work doing house to house enquiries. One striking observation emerged from this which must have made the officers sanguine about finding some kind of lead. A man had been seen walking slowly down Ling Lane late at night. A witness noted that he had been behaving as if he did not want to be seen, and he had a 'slouching gait'. If this was the killer, he would have seen Ann Barker's lamplight and naturally, if he went to chase this up, he would have found himself in a place where he could take advantage. The search widened, and nothing more came of the sighting.

Servicemen Suspects

The investigation then switched to the one notable feature of the immediate vicinity that might have led to questions being asked: there was a hostel for Polish servicemen on nearby Wetherby Road. The primary material evidence needed was of course the inevitably bloodstained clothing that the killer would have. But the task of interviewing so many foreign workmen was gargantuan; interpreters were called in from Leeds University, but there were difficulties in the dynamics of the whole communication process.

Most irritating for the detectives was the fact that, contrary to expectations, the Polish workmen had a lot of clothes, and had tended to throw away old clothes. It wasn't simply a case of looking at everyone's minimal and functional basic wardrobe.

Fundamentally, what was the motive for the killing? Ann Barker was not wealthy. She had no hidden life, no secret habits or enemies. It had all the hallmarks of being an opportunist crime: the kind of assault a desperate stranger might commit, thinking that the woman was wealthy and had cash around the house. One sure fact is that in 1948 Ling Lane would have been difficult to supervise and police by a neighbourhood watch scheme – even such unofficial vigilance. It is a very long road and quite wide. There is considerable space around the dwellings, even today. If a silent killer did arrive and took her life for supposed gain, then it would have been a simple matter to do the deed. Noise would not have carried. It was winter and the night was dark. Maybe the man slouching down the lane sensed easy prey.

Theories?

One final pathetic detail is the fact that the home where this terrible act happened was called Rose Cottage – just the kind of traditionally-pastoral name one might give to a rural retreat. Now it is a name full of awful irony. Even today, a walk along that restful road gives a sense of space and tranquillity: a passer-by would never dream of such an atrocity taking place there. It is the kind of murder case that invites amateur sleuths to speculate. The most likely lines of thought regarding the nature of the murder might be these:

• The opportunist: passing and seeing here was a lonely woman with no 'defensible space', as a police officer or a sociologist might have called it, and going in for an easy theft.

• A planned attack: as Ann had a gun, was there a fear based on a previous incident? Maybe an intruder had returned, but this was still an individual approach.

• The area was a rich one (and still is) so gangs would know of affluent houses there ('millionaire's belt' is how some Leeds people refer to places just a few miles away).

• The so-called psychopath, selecting vulnerable victims.

We are left with that most frustrating personage of crime history – the unknown villain. Now 59 years have passed since this terrible killing.

Henry Warner Murder

Very soon after Ann Barker was killed, another murder happened in Leeds, this time in the city centre. Again, the villain was never traced.

Today, as you turn left from Leeds railway station into Wellington Street, you have a distant prospect of every possible symbol of the 'New Leeds': new businesses, building work in progress and a redesigned pedestrian-friendly part of the city. But in the dark days after World War Two there was something of a crime wave in the northern cities and towns, and the robberies and attacks were mostly against businesses. The most vulnerable were the small ones. Leafing through the newspapers from the years c.1946–56, it is difficult to miss the number of attacks that nowadays would be called 'heists' in Hollywood crime movies.

But one unsolved murder of the time and in that street off the railway station is far from glamorous. It was a savage attack on an old, defenceless man, protecting his own premises. He was beaten with a hard, blunt instrument at his shop early in March, and he was still unconscious in hospital almost a week later, struggling for life. Before he died, police officers were sitting at his bedside, hoping for a recovery and some words that might lead to an arrest, or at least to a suspect. But he died without recovering consciousness, and an inquest was held on 19 March.

The Attack

Warner was 77 years old, a portmanteau repairer; he was found unconscious on the floor of his shop with deep head wounds. He was discovered by two men around 10.30 in the morning, and he had been seen alive an hour earlier by a Miss Battle, working at her kiosk. The coroner, Dr Swanton, stated that this had been 'a calculated and inhuman assault on an old and industrious citizen'.

Superintendent Bowman of Leeds CID asked the public for help. Scotland Yard were involved; a photograph of the time shows four detectives hurriedly going down to the basement of the shop in Wellington Street, a sense of urgency in their movement.

The first momentous discovery was that of a large steel bar wrapped in brown paper. It was a packing-case opener, and police were sure it had been used in the attack. There was also a lead concerning a woman

Wellington Street, close to the shops.

wearing black, seen in the street during that time. The most promising lead, though, came from two passengers in a passing tram. At that time there was a large central bus station just a short way further down Wellington Street from Warner's shop, and both buses and trams were always busy on that route – it was the main way to Armley and to the Park Lane area.

A new blue-type tram, number 173, was the one the witnesses were probably on. Many people would have been on board at that time, bound for work in most cases. It comes as no surprise that one passenger saw something of great interest, but she described the woman who had been sitting next to her, and on her right, with a view directly out of the window. Police desperately wanted to contact the other passenger, as she would have been facing the shop (and trams did not move very quickly). All they knew was that two men had been seen on the pavement outside the shop at about the right time: they were loitering.

Frustration in the Enquiry

But the woman never came forward. Chief Constable Barpett wanted some help in what he called a 'gruesome' case. The most hopeful development seemed to be to trace the makers of the brown paper wrapping, and so a series of interviews with such manufacturers took place. It was also thought that there might be a link with a killing in Bramley three years previously, the victim being a Mrs Nichols. But nothing was substantial in that.

Unsolved

Little chubby-faced Henry Warner, who wore pince-nez spectacles and looked like everyone's friendly grandfather, had been murdered and everyone was stumped. He had been based down in the cellar area, always a tough space to defend if cornered and open to intruders. The Warner case is typical of that brand of murder taking place in a busy thoroughfare, and in working hours, when there ought to be plenty of witnesses, but nothing palpable emerged in the investigation. It was a bold, heartless robbery and murder, leaving an old man to die a long and painful death. The city of Leeds was suitably outraged, and people tried to help, but in the end no witnesses were found and no leads established that might have proved successful. Everyone hates an unsolved killing of course, and in that period, when the war had left large numbers of criminals with guns from military service use, there was gun crime and violence increasing everywhere. Leeds was rich in small businesses, often run by older people and in places with no protective barrier nor even with a supporting, supervisory person available. It must have been easy money for the brutal types on the lookout for a full till and a weak shopkeeper.

THIRTY-THREE

Short Stories 1: Strange People

'Curiouser and curiouser'
Lewis Carroll

The Davenport Brothers

'A bad turn' might best describe these unfortunate entertainers, who in 1865, when ordinary folk expected their money's worth after hard-earned cash was spent in the theatre, were in dire straits in Leeds. They managed to give their performance to a small audience at the music hall, but trouble was brewing all the way through. People knew that they had failed to turn up in Hull just before this and also at Huddersfield.

The Davenports' act was a séance, and that was always a risky business. Part of their act involved them being tied up and reef knots were used. In Leeds they objected to those knots being used and there was dissatisfaction expressed loudly. Let the newspaper of the time tell the main event: 'They alleged that the two gentlemen who were tying them were pulling the knots too tight and were injuring them; a scene of great excitement ensued and the two brothers hastily left the hall, and neither the inducement of their friend nor that of any other person was powerful enough to bring them back.'

The men who had trussed them mightily were Adjutant Longbolton of the Leeds Engineer Rifle Corps and Sergeant McArthur of the Royal Engineers. There was even a surgeon there to be referee. But none of these men could prevent the riot that followed the brothers' escape. Their cabinet and all their equipment was smashed to pieces by the disgruntled crowd. After the police had been called there was a loud demonstration, and a local 'speculator' – the man who had booked the brothers – was forced to arrange for the crowd to have their money returned. He apparently agreed to do so, but it was never actually done and he played for time. As the local reporter wrote, 'It need hardly be added that the performances arranged for Saturday were not attempted…The stretching was not very agreeable to the brothers, and it was the general impression of the audience that they wanted to do the stretching themselves, this being one of the means by which they made their performance successful.'

Foster Powell the Walking Phenomenon

In the 18th century walking was a highly popular way of getting from place to place. People would walk immense distances and think nothing of it. The poet Wordsworth would walk over 20 miles in a day and then more if he had to get back home. But even this pales into insignificance when compared with the achievements of Foster Powell of Horsforth. He was born there in 1734 but moved to London to start a career in law. He worked for a certain Mr Bingley, and it was while he was with this gentleman that his pedestrian feats began, because he promised him that he could walk 50 miles on the road to Bath in seven hours. In 1764 he did exactly that, doing the first 10 miles in one hour.

He did not stop at that. He decided to walk great stretches of open land in Switzerland and France; in 1773 he walked from London to York and back again in five days and four hours – a walk of 400 miles. This he did to win some cash in a bet.

He then graduated to running and managed to do two miles in 10 minutes; we can only speculate as to exactly what he could achieve if he was around today, with a coach, designer equipment and specialist diets. Then off he went on the Bath road again, and this time he did 100 miles in a solid day's non-stop walking. But London to York was his favourite, so he did it again in six days that time and then again in 1792. By that time he was 58 years old, and he was out to beat his own record. He made it in five days and just under 16 hours. According to a report on this, he was welcomed on his return 'with loud huzzas of the astonished and anxious spectators'.

Foster always wanted new challenges and adapted to sprinting as well, running one mile and walking another in 15 minutes, which he did with no problems and hardly breaking into a sweat. When he really stretched himself and took on something he just could not do, he lost the bet, but actually his friends raised money for him by subscription and he came out of it well. An example of this was when he walked from London to Canterbury but took the wrong road and got lost.

Foster had no time for wealth really: he never earned more than £10 in one time. The secret of his success appears to have been in his frugal lifestyle and eating only light food. A Victorian journal describes him in this way:

> 'He seems to have considered his wonderful agility as a circumstance from which he derived great glory. In person he was tall and thin, about five feet nine inches, very strong downwards, well calculated for walking, and rather of a sallow complexion, in disposition he was mild and gentle and possessed many valuable qualifications.'

He was usually careful and restrained, but unfortunately his obsession finally killed him: he overdid things in his last York walk and pushed himself too far. He only let himself have five hours' rest in the whole return journey. He was seriously ill, with a sudden collapse in 1793, and he died on 15 April that year.

His funeral was a major event in London: 'The funeral was characteristically a walking one, from New Inn, through Fleet Street and up Ludgate Hill...The attendants were all men of respectability.' Here was one of the many great eccentrics spawned by the city of Leeds, and we have to wonder why he never walked there, from London to his home town.

Woodbine Lizzie

Many Leeds folk alive today have vivid memories of the Leeds character Woodbine Lizzie. She was a regular sight in the city centre in the 1950s, smoking a Woodbine cigarette with a bag over her arm, unwashed and unkempt. Her real name was Alice Porter. Nowadays she would undoubtedly have the phrase 'Bag Lady' applied to her. But her fame must have spread very widely because during World War Two an army transporter was called 'Woodbine Lizzie from Leeds'.

Members of my own family recall her, as on one occasion two Wades were looking in Lewis's shop window when they became aware of a figure standing behind them. It was Lizzie, and in her posh voice she said, 'Don't they look a right sight that lot?' Another memory, posted on a website by John Hitchen, recalls her chopping wood, and Mr Hitchen says she looked like 'Old Mother Riley in the movies.'

John Morgan, in his book *A Celebration of Leeds*, notes that the legendary story about her is that she was the unwanted daughter of a lord of the realm, disowned at birth. She is fixed in Leeds mythology and street history as the woman cadging 'Woodies' as she tramped the streets.

The Blind Botanist

In 1920 John Grimshaw Wilkinson was interviewed by a *Times* reporter. Wilkinson had been discussed in the recent prestigious Royal Institution lecture by Professor Bragg, so the journalist went to see the minor celebrity. The man had been blind since he was 22, and he was 64 when interviewed. The Leeds man was self-taught in science, particularly in botany.

He was a grocer by trade, but his passion was plants, and on one occasion, when taken to Temple Newsam by a friend, he showed that just by touching a tree he could name the variety. 'If I feel a poppy leaf,' he said, 'On a hot July morning it feels cold, but if I feel a leaf of London Pride at the same time it is quite warm, although the plants may be within a yard of each other. When I touch anything I note whether it is warm or cold and then I ask myself why.' During heavy showers he became aware that trees made different sounds. He told the reporter that the oak was the noisiest in a storm as it 'reflected the echoes by its leaves'.

Wilkinson's claims were quite stunning, especially in relation to touch. Not only did he say that it was a 'delight' to shake hands with some people (and he talked about a Leeds surgeon whose handshake was nervous but who could 'handle the lancet with great skill'), but then he extended this interest with a reference to prisoners in Armley, saying that if he were allowed to go to that gaol, he would shake hands with the prisoners and 'at once tell which were the habitual criminals and which were not'. He explained that criminals would not be 'well balanced in action'.

There had to be something substantial and interesting in all this, as Mr Wilkinson was given a master of science degree by the University of Leeds. This remarkable man fits in well with a long line of self-taught types around Leeds: it appears to be a place that nurtures this faculty. But whatever the reasons for Mr Wilkinson developing his extraordinary powers, the point is that he did so with a scientific curiosity and a careful method of enquiry, matching his analytical mind with the strange creativity in his insights into nature. The results were astounding at times, and we have to wish that he had indeed been allowed into Armley Gaol for his innovative experiments. Who knows what kind of studies that may have opened up.

At the time there was no one bold enough to take him up on the offer. But one feels that he would have had the confidence to impress anyone monitoring his progress with the villains.

YORKSHIRE ODDITIES,

INCIDENTS,

AND

STRANGE EVENTS.

BY

S. BARING-GOULD, M.A.,

AUTHOR OF "CURIOUS MYTHS OF THE MIDDLE AGES,"
"ICELAND: ITS SCENES AND SAGAS—THE BOOK OF WERE-WOLVES,"
ETC.

―――――――――――

" There be such a company of wilful gentlemen within Yorkshire as there be not in all
England besides."—*Abbot of York to Cromwell*, 1556, *Rolls House MS.*

―――――――――――

VOL. II.

JOHN HODGES,
46, BEDFORD STREET, STRAND, LONDON.
1874.

One of the first
collections of
strange tales.

THIRTY-FOUR

Short Stories 2: Strong Characters

'Hands that the rod of Empire might have swayed
Or waked to ecstasy the living lyre.'
Thomas Gray

Vesta Victoria

In 1958 a theatre reviewer wrote 'Miss Violette de Saxe as Vesta Victoria' when he reviewed a performance of old time music hall at the Metropolitan, Edgeware Road. Vesta Victoria had died seven years before the event, but it was the ultimate tribute to the star from Leeds who had given the world such songs as *Daddy Wouldn't Buy me a Bow Wow* and *Now I have to Call him Father*.

She was born in Leeds on 26 November 1873 and was on stage when she was just a baby, playing the young Queen Victoria. Then, at the Cambridge Music Hall in London, she made her debut proper at the age of 10. She performed at every important music hall venue as the years went by.

According to one writer, she was 'a pleasant-faced, rather plump, fair-haired woman, with a low-pitched voice and specialised in character songs in which she usually presented herself as the victim of some misfortune...' In performance she was usually in bedraggled clothes and gave everything to the delivery of a personality in a semi-comic and semi-tragic situation. She retired quite early, in comparative terms, around 1918, but she did return once, in 1926, and after that she became a legend. In any discussion of the great days of music hall, Vesta Victoria has to be mentioned.

Hancock and Markham

Leeds can claim a major part in the fight to bring good money and working conditions to houseworkers, something very important particularly in the years after World War Two. In 1946 the Minister of Labour commissioned a report on the training of women for domestic work. Two Leeds women, Florence Hancock and Violet Markham, got to work on the task, and their report brought about the foundation of the National Institute of Houseworkers. In 1951 a centre of that organisation opened in Chapeltown, at 53 Mount Street.

Before this, the nature of housework had been well down the league tables of women's work, and it was in need of pride, status and respect, as well as a structure for proper training. All this came along thanks to women like the two Leeds pioneers. Professional training was introduced and women who came through the course gained a diploma. Then, as graduates went into the work place, they were supported and backup always provided. The training was given at regional centres, such as the one in Chapeltown, and there is a memoir written by Christine Nolan to testify to the excellence of this new provision. Christine points out that the organisation even had its own magazine, *The Houseworker,* and she quotes a report written in 1949 describing one of the main virtues of this innovation:

> 'The setting up of Daily Houseworker services has shown that in a most varied group of towns experienced workers are willing to come forward to take the examination for the Diploma in order that they may be employed under conditions of a guaranteed week with the Daily Houseworkers Service and the institute behind them...'

Joe Fox

Sports people have been largely absent from these pages, but now mention must be made of the talented and very successful boxer of the years following World War One, Joe Fox. He was born in 1894 and became a professional when only 16. Joe Fox went from a lowly beginning in fairground booths to eventually become the Featherweight Champion of Great Britain.

He was always adventurous and highly motivated, going across the

Atlantic to join up with his brothers, and that when he was just 20. There he started touring and his natural ability brought favourable responses from the crowds in New York and elsewhere. He and his brothers even went as far as Australia in this work. When it came to his top fights, though, Joe won a Lonsdale Belt at bantamweight and went on to fight at featherweight, taking the championship in 1921 after defeating Mike Honeyman.

Fighters have their ups and downs, and Joe lost a fight he never should have done: he had won the first 12 rounds on points when he fought Eugene Criquie a year after his title, only to lose after receiving the proverbial 'sucker punch' from the opponent. Of course, boxing attracts a lot of gambling, and in those days it was one of the most lucrative ways to invest for a sportsman; Joe must have looked a hot favourite on paper and his Leeds supporters backed him heavily. They must have been hugely disappointed to see that lucky swipe hit home on their man's chin.

John Nelson, Methodist Charisma

Nelson was born in 1707 at Birstall. He was a friend and lay assistant of John Wesley, being converted to Methodism when he joined a crowd listening to the Methodist founder preach in London. He was a stonemason by trade but became a powerful and influential speaker around Leeds, where he gained the title 'pioneer of Methodism in Yorkshire'. His journal is a standard Methodist text and has been instrumental in spreading the thoughts and ideas of that faith. When he heard Wesley speak at Moorfields, he expressed the profound impact it had on him in his journal: 'As soon as he got up upon the stand, he stroked back his hair, and turned his face towards where I stood...His countenance struck such an awful dread upon me before I heard him speak, that it made my heart beat like the pendulum of a clock...'

But Nelson himself was no mean preacher. He was persecuted and reviled in his time, but his verbal power is evidenced in a tale about him preaching in Grimsby, when the vicar there hired a drummer to drum out Nelson's voice. The preacher was not deterred and carried on, and the tale is that the drummer stopped and was 'cut to the heart by what he had heard'. He threw away the drum and listened. Nelson also brought Methodism to Farsley and Pudsey. But it was not all smooth sailing for him. On one journey, coming from York, he was attacked and felled when a massive brick was thrown at him. He was helped and treated, then rode on, and he was again attacked. Amazingly, he still carried on the next day towards Osmotherley.

Leeds became a major centre of Methodism, and its beginning is due to Nelson. What happened was that a certain William Shent, who was a barber in Leeds, went to listen to Nelson in Armley. He was deeply affected and changed his allegiance to the Methodist cause. He and some friends then initiated the Leeds 'connexion' and talked with Wesley himself in 1743 in Briggate.

May Thompson

Businessman Frank Temple Thompson's second marriage was to the most vibrant May Campbell, but she was to become known in the music world as May Thompson, and she has to be one of Leeds's most celebrated musicians and songwriters. In 1921 an accident had caused irreparable damage to her back which meant she always had to use a stick to walk, but she still appeared on stage with Leeds amateur companies on several occasions. It is in composition that her reputation lies, though.

May wrote a ballad called *A Four Leaf Clover* and that made her mark; later in 1934 she met the great Gracie Fields and wrote for her, and in a film called *Love, Life and Laughter* one of May's songs was included. She had arrived. The song was recorded by well-known dance bands. She started to move in film and music industry circles, so that all kinds of stars came to Leeds and visited the Thompsons at Bramhope, including Sidney Howerd, Charles Laughton and the hugely popular composer Ivor Novello.

The couple were a formidable combination: Frank owned the Harehills Picture House, and so the pair presented to Leeds and to the wider circles in the entertainment business a wonderful mix of talent and glamour. He was always very smart and loved entertaining. May clearly had a talent that could adapt to almost any audience, progressing from her first songs, written for children, to film music. Thanks to these two, there were some colourful occasions and plenty of creativity around Leeds in the 1930s, to counteract the desperate times of slump and 'the dole'.

Beryl Burton

Beryl, arguably one of the sportswomen with one of the greatest lists of achievements, was born in Morley in 1937, and cycling was her passion. Twice she took the Women's World Road Race Championship Trophy (in 1960 and in 1967). Beryl also took the Women's World Pursuit Championship five times between 1959 and 1966, and she won the silver medal three times and the bronze medal three times in the 1960s. Perhaps her most stunning achievement, though, was to win the Best All-Rounder 'Open' for no less than 25 years between 1959 and 1983.

What will certainly stand out in the record books is her record for the 12-hour time trial – a distance of just over 277 miles (beating the men's record). The biking life is a tough and dangerous one; she was hit several times by cars, in spite of her garish colours, and her chances of beating a record were ruined once when a driver cut her up. But there was more controversy than that. When she was beaten by her daughter in the 1976 Road Race event, her mood must have shown because in *The People* newspaper the headline appeared 'Bike Ace Beryl Snubs Daughter.'

Beryl wrote an autobiography called *Personal Best* in 1968, and some of the memories there give us the best insight into her tenacity as well as her thorough professionalism. An example is this passage, in which she copes with the shock of seeing that her research on the route in France had worked out and she expresses her sheer enthusiasm:

'I could concentrate on my ride. At every intersection on the route the police were blowing their whistles as only the gendarmerie can, warning others of my approach. Some of them looked surprised, as if they were not expecting me so soon. The assurances about the road-works, the mud and the pipe-laying had been justified. They had all mysteriously disappeared overnight…and I zipped on, my legs feeling fluent, the rain holding off. I could not engage the big sprocket and engaged the second chain-ring once or twice on some hills.'

In a search for a Leeds icon, we need look no further than Beryl. She died in action, riding her bike, when her heart failed on 8 May 1996. Perhaps the main aspect of her career – one that makes the heart sink even now – was that her own local newspaper let her down. She notes '*The Yorkshire Evening Post,* consistent as usual, gave a passing mention in about three lines at the foot of a column, to my achievement...' She had just won a major trophy and had enjoyed, as she put it, '25 years at the top'. Maybe some of our media need to recall just how important it is to remind readers that there are sports other than football. Cycling, along with many others, has had to fight hard for coverage, and Beryl helped to bring this issue to light.

She was a wonderful sportswoman, with courage, athleticism, professional dedication, and she was an inspiration to younger people. Of course, she would have to be charged with obsession, but then that seems to come with success. Her successes were phenomenal in her chosen field, and her name will always be in the record books – and never forgotten in Leeds, we can bet on that. There must have been hot competition for space in her trophy cabinet at home, but polishing them had to be a pleasure.

John Deakin Heaton

Heaton, son of a Leeds bookseller, became one of the most highly-respected medical men in the mid-Victorian years, being physician to the Leeds general Infirmary in 1850 and a medical fellow of University College just a year before that. His education as a doctor was remarkable for the age: he went from Leeds Grammar School to Leeds School of Medicine, but then gained valuable experience first in Paris and then in other parts of Europe. On coming back to Leeds, he went into general practice, but, as with most scientists of his time, he had wider interests and also lectured on botany and *materia medica* at the school.

But why Leeds has kept his memory alive is mainly due to his important role in founding the Yorkshire College, precursor of the university. The roots of this achievement were in his active role in the Yorkshire Board of Education, and he was also a member of the first school board for the borough. In 1869 a committee was put together with the aim of taking steps to found a college. The principal aim was, as one study of 1880 put it, 'for the purpose of giving advanced instruction in the sciences applicable to the industrial arts'. The college was inaugurated in 1875 and in 1880 an essayist wrote that the results of this had been very important: 'It is already established as one of the permanent institutions of the district, with its own estate and buildings, and what is

Hotel Metropole, the grace
and style of Leeds 'culture'.

much more, a comparatively large staff of able and cultured Professors is living among us and leavening society more than it may at first recognise...'

Heaton's influence did not end in Leeds either: he was made a Citizen of London, mainly because the Clothworkers Company of the City of London had recieved such a spin-off benefit from what he had achieved in Leeds within their industry. Heaton was one of those characters you would want on any group assembled to get the sleeves rolled up and get something done.

Denis Healey and Douglas Gabb

The present writer almost had an influence on modern British history when, in the year 1959, he rushed excitedly, with a band of mates from Osmondthorpe County Secondary Modern School on a visit to the Houses of Parliament, to meet Mr Denis Healey, MP for South East Leeds. We slammed into him and almost knocked him off his feet and into the Thames. I recall him laughing. That was the type of man he was. Healey was a character, larger than life, and he served Leeds well, though he was brought up in Keighley.

His media image may have been one of a bluff, well-informed man with bushy eyebrows, but there was nothing shallow about him. He was a fine intellect and had the ability to understand and act on that particular kind of process in which a community changes for the better. From the first, he attributed much of his success in Leeds to Gabb, his agent and also at one time Mayor of Leeds. What Healey says about Gabb explains the rapport and sense of empathy they had:

> 'We have grown up together in the constituency, and I have learned much from him. He was born in the poorest part of the city; his mother was an usher at the local theatre and he saw little of his father, who was a soldier. He never forgot the humiliation of being made to stand in front of a class while his teacher described him as an object of charity...'

This was the boy who became a remarkable man, at first being trained for a career as a jockey at Newmarket and then going on to be involved in engineering, including spending time at the Royal Ordnance Factory in Leeds. Healey points out that Douglas Gabb put in huge amounts of time and energy for the Labour Party unpaid, as well as being agent for Denis. Gabb even used to work part-time as a milkman to make ends meet.

The Leeds Healey first knew was still a place with terrible industrial pollution problems. He writes in his autobiography about these darker elements of Leeds life: 'The population exploded, from 15,000 to 207,000 in the 100 years to 1861, then doubling again in the next 50. Charles Dickens described Leeds as the beastliest place, one of the nastiest I know…The housing was appalling, the dirt indescribable.' Until the Clean Air Act of 1956 it was still one of the smokiest towns in Europe.

When I was aged about 10, in 1958 or so, I was travelling home from the centre of Leeds to Whitkirk. The bus had to stop absolutely still for a long time as a yellowy smog closed in. We all sat on the bus, unable to move in that enveloping, thick-soupy consistency of gas and chemicals, in a strange purgatory of nothingness. That was the Leeds Healey had first known. But, as he pointed out, it was also a cultural place where you could see major plays before they opened in London.

Denis Healey had the kind of impact we rarely see from politicians here: a real presence in debate, well informed and with an air of authority. Douglas Gabb was, in my opinion, a man who represented the essence of Leeds graft and determination, with a dash of vision to sustain him. Healey was also well aware of the results of huge industries folding. He wrote about the closure of Barn Bow, when the Tories sold it to Vickers: 'So unemployment on the council estates of East Leeds became exceptionally high. The service industries which took up some of the slack created by the decline of manufacturing did not require the old skills which the government had made redundant.'

As one reviewer said about Healey, he was 'rumbustious and full of fun', but he was also a character Leeds valued and found to be dedicated to the place and people.

THIRTY-FIVE

A Chapter of Accidents

'Build me straight, oh worthy master,
Staunch and strong, a goodly vessel
That shall laugh at all disaster
And with wave and whirlwind wrestle.'
(Longfellow)

A Drowning at Gledhow, 1865

On a Monday afternoon in 1865, about 150 people were skating on a huge pond at Gledhow on a large estate owned by a man called Cooper. The pond was 500 yards by 100 yards in dimensions, and the owner of the place was quite happy for all and sundry to come and use it. After large numbers had already used it on this fateful day, Mary Jane Balmer, just 16 years old, came to join in the fun, some young medical students being with her.

There was an assistant of her father (a surgeon) with her to keep an eye on things, but some fun started when a chair, in the possession of the medical students, was pushed out onto the ice. A student called George Broughton pushed Mary Jane's sister, and then Mary Jane herself, around on this chair. But when they were around 12 yards from the edge, the ice broke and the water where they were was about 14-feet deep. Mary Jane and a man of 28, Lyndon Smith, went down under the water.

Several people present tried hard to save them; it was Broughton who had shoved Mary Jane into the danger area, but then to his credit he went in after her. The newspaper report of the time said:

'His head could be seen above the water, but he was lost because the ice kept breaking whenever he attempted to get out. Mr G. Broughton fell into the water at the same time as Miss Balmer, but his brother retrieved him with a stick...all the twenty or so persons on the ice at the time disappeared...'

Broughton tried hard to help anyone he could. At one point a hand came up through the broken ice and he did his best to help, but it was all in vain.

But, of course, no one had considered the possibility of an accident. It was a carefree atmosphere. There were no ropes or long pieces of wood present for such an event. But after some time, two men called Rhodes and Naylor stripped and went in, seeing the increasingly desperate situation. The reporter who spoke to one of them later noted that the man thought during the ordeal that he had a body in his grasp, but it turned out to be a coat. The place where the bodies had gone down was discussed and considered to be the most dangerous part of the pond.

It was 90 minutes after the two people went down that the bodies were finally recovered; the coroner said at the inquest that there had been 'no precipitancy or rashness on the part of Mr Broughton' and the poor man had done all he could to save young Mary Jane. There was strong advice about ropes and poles being placed at the ready for the next time skating might happen at Cooper's pool.

Leeds was full of talk about the story for some time. A letter was written to *The Times* two days after the tragedy, in which a person signed as 'Jaques' wrote 'I am led to suggest the following simple and cheap precaution for all semi-public skating places.' His solution was a plank. That may not have been revolutionary but he was sure of the benefits, 'Let a plank of deal, 11 inches wide and 17 or 18 feet long, be placed at or near the pond...In the event of a break in the ice the plank is shoved across the fracture and affords safe support to those succouring and those immersed.'

All very wise, but too late to help poor Mary Jane and Lyndon Smith.

Blackburn's Yard Explosion

In 1838 some almshouses were constructed on Holbeck Moor. They were not made because some local philanthropist had money to spare, but as a result of extreme need following a massive disaster.

The 1830s were a dark period in the history of the working class. Not only was there a problem with the price of food – it was very high – but there were Chartist actions and a spate of crimes in rural areas. On top of all that, in Holbeck there was a massive explosion in Blackburn's Yard, as a firework-maker's factory blew up.

The power of the blast was so intense that windows and doors all across Leeds shook and shivered – it must have seemed to some folk that the end of the world was nigh. But in fact the tragedy happened because Susannah Dockray blew out a candle. She did so, thoughtlessly, in the room where the gunpowder was stored. Before any really noisy blast disrupted anyone, the poor girl ran out into the yard, her frock on fire, to a background of crackling noises.

Then other young women joined in the panic and ran out with Susannah, but we have to wonder at a Mrs Wood because she scrambled back into the danger zone, perhaps hoping to stop things escalating to the point at which the whole place would be blown to hell. But she was too late. The factory was splattered into fragments in the Holbeck air. Of course, Mrs Wood was killed, along with her child. Other places nearby suffered extreme damage as well. Members of families around the factory were fortunate that they were not in vulnerable positions when the explosion happened: James Walker, for instance, was buried under a pile of rubble. Other people did die, however, including a man of 70.

The Boiler Went up in Smoke
In 1866 in Dewsbury Road, two men died as a result of a boiler explosion at the Frogland Mungo Works. Casualties were high in addition to the deaths, as 18 women were also maimed. The engineman was Samuel Pearson and the rag machine tenter was Benjamin Preston; they took quite a while to die, passing away in hospital the day after the disaster. What the coroner and the papers wanted to know was whether there was any suspicion that the boiler was faulty in any way.

The men had died in agony. Pearson had serious burns on his face and body and Preston had a compound fracture of his left thigh bone. What remained when their manner of death was described and surgeons had asked about actions taken, was to start an enquiry about the boiler's condition, and so the court initiated the process, initially with two engineers being employed to test the place and look at the evidence. The court was adjourned until that was done and results given. Some of the men who reported later were of very good professional standing, such as Mr Manning of the Institute of Mechanical Engineers. The worst fears were to be confirmed.

The Yorkshire Post explained the nature of the problem that had caused the explosion: 'The fixed load upon the small valve was not excessive, supposing the boiler to have been in good condition. He (Mr Manning) had no hesitation in saying that the explosion was caused by the weakening of the boiler by the secret extensive corrosion.' What should have been done, it was commented, was that there should have been a period inspection, but these matters were not so strictly enforced then. Even more paradoxical by today's standards, the matters relating to safe maintenance of such fixtures and plant was sidelined, as a story emerged about one Joshua Goodall lighting his pipe.

The verdict was accidental death. Nothing came from statements given by tradesmen about noted leaks and malfunctions of the boiler, which was, it was claimed, just five years old. The Health and Safety Executive of 2007 would be shivering with indignation should they read this.

A Lucky Escape

The Victorian period was also the time when poisons were not really handled and regulated with much care and attention. Often children and servants would collect medicines and be open to getting things wrong. In a Bradford case in which poison was accidentally mixed into a recipe for making boiled sweets, the deaths went into double figures. Sometimes the errors were down to illiteracy and quantities were wrongly prepared. In one case in Leeds, Mr Haigh was lucky not to die as a result of a mistake.

In 1868 he took some laudanum, which he thought was tincture of rhubarb. A neighbour of Mr Haigh, called Barnes, had died as a result of taking the mixture from the very same bottle that Haigh drank from. What had happened was that Barnes had a problem with diarrhoea and the tincture was to put that right. A handbook of remedies of that time states that rhubarb 'is given internally for diarrhoea' and that 'one to four drachms' should be given as a tincture for a 'debilitated state of the bowels'. Mr Barnes thought he was having exactly that, but he died.

Barnes, as the doctor's report made clear, had died from diarrhoea, 'the deceased having ejected laudanum from his stomach'. The cause of the death and near-death was in the incompetence of a young assistant, who had carelessly filled the bottle with laudanum instead of the rhubarb tincture.

Horribly Painful Death of a Child
In industrial Leeds in these perilous years of the mid-Victorian times, children were always especially vulnerable when adults were going about the daily grind. Young Jane Scatchard and her subsequent fate are a nasty example of this: she was simply walking past the Anchor of Hope Inn in Leylands when the landlord, Mr Woodson, decided to wash his barrels. Little Jane was only five years old, and she thought that this would be a good place to play, so she took hold of a barrel but then fell in – the water was scalding hot. She fell into the water head first.

The girl suffered intense agony for four hours before she died of the burns. *The Leeds Mercury* reported that 'The jury, in returning a verdict of accidental death severely censured Mr Woodson for washing his barrels in the public footpath, a thing which Mr Emsley [coroner] said was against the law, and must not be repeated.'

In those years, when factories, shops and all kinds of industries were being made and set out in all kinds of haphazard ways, with no thoughts but for the efficiency of the production process, Leeds people were living on the edge, exposed to all kinds of noxious vapours, chemicals and noises. They would spend their working days in intense noise, breathing in effluents; they would risk being at the mercy of some incompetent professionals in the health services and they would face dangers every time they were in any built-up area. Often, their medicine was as dangerous as the illness they had, and employers could subject them to high-risk activities without proper protection. The years of the Victorian heyday of industry were certainly years of living dangerously.

Of course, families grew wiser to all this as they were more involved in the world of work and were getting an education. Better levels of literacy obviously helped people to become aware of the whole range of potential dangers lurking in the workplace and indeed in the home. Public health had improved by those last decades of the century, but the workplace was still packed with danger.

Many of the real 'heroes' of the city are surely unknown now, because they were the people in everyday work who fought to improve these things and to have some kind of justice and fairness in their work within these perilous places. Some of them, such as mines, would not really be regulated and controlled for some time to come at this time of Victorian prosperity – a prosperity that was often built on high risk and great danger to the individuals caught up in that huge industrial state, feeding and supplying not just England but her vast Empire across the map that was painted red.

Cold, Not Machines or Smog

Then there was the effects of the sheer threats and harrowing suffering brought about by nothing at all connected to the Industrial Revolution, such as the death of Matilda Wormald, aged only 28. Matilda had been living what her father described as an 'irregular life' – that is, she left home and had been on her own in various places. In early January 1880 she went to the home of Eliza Gee in Mabgate and asked her for a bed for the night. Eliza, co-habiting and not married, managed to accommodate her. But poor Matilda was so ill the next day that Eliza let her stay for most of the week.

Matilda went on, clearly very feeble and at the end of her tether, and she was then seen by another woman called Wormald, whose partner was rather more callous than the previous men, saying 'You will not have to stay here', followed by his action of actually turfing her out into the street with the words 'We will not have you here any more.' This was at least how it was according to one witness, but Wormald denied it, saying that he told the woman he could not afford to keep her there.

Matilda Wormald was found dead in a deserted house. The local paper described what happened: 'On Friday afternoon police constable Watmuff was called to the house, number 70 Mabgate at present unoccupied, where he saw a woman named Matilda Wormald, apparently in a dying state. The officer sent to Millgarth station and Mr Hollingworth, one of the police surgeons, was telegraphed for but when he arrived life was extinct. The body was removed to the mortuary…'

She had pneumonia, technically lobar pneumonia, and doctors then could do nothing about it. What most upset the jury at the coroner's court was the 'cruel treatment meted out to the dying woman'.

Bibliography

Heroes

Books

A Celebration of Leeds, Yorkshire Evening Post Leeds centenary, 1993

Briggs, Asa *Victorian Cities* Penguin, 1968

Golden Years of Leeds True North Books, Elland, 2000

Hattersley, Roy *Lives Remembered The Times*/Blewbury, 1993

Hunt, Tristram *Building Jerusalem: the rise and fall of the Victorian city* Phoenix, 2005

Moore, Emily Jane *The Life and Reign of Queen Victoria* Nicholson, 1900

Morgan, John *A Celebration of Leeds Yorkshire Post*, 2006

Progress and Commerce, 1893 The London Printing and Engraving Company, 1893 (The *Yorkshire* volume in the series)

Tate, Lynne Stevenson *Aspects of Leeds 3* Wharncliffe, 2001

Journals and periodicals

Appeal Court Records

Leeds Mercury

Old Yorkshire

Times Digital Archive

Thoresby Society Miscellany

Yorkshire Post

Villains

Chapman, Pauline *Madame Tussaud's Chamber of Horrors, two hundred years of gruesome murder* Grafton, 1988

Davies, Owen *Murder, Magic, Madness: The Victorian Trials of Dove and The wizard* Pearson Longman, 2005

Fielding, Steve *Pierrepoint: A Family of Executioners* John Blake, 2006

Goodman, David *Foul Deeds and Suspicious Deaths in Leeds* Wharncliffe, 2003

Lavelle, Patrick *Shadow of the Ripper* John Blake, 2003

Shore, W. Teignmouth *Trials of Charles Peace* Hodge and Co., 1926

Thomas, Donald *Villains' Paradise: Britain's underworld from the spivs to the Krays* John Murray, 2005

Van der Elst, Violet *On the Gallows* The author, London, 1937

Wilkinson, George Theodore *The Newgate Calendar* Sphere, 1992

Victims

Barnard, Sylvia *Viewing the Breathless Corpse: coroners and inquests in Victorian Leeds* Words@Woodmere, 2001

Best, Geoffrey *Mid Victorian Britain 1851–75* Fontana, 1988

Bland, James *The Complete True Crime Diaries, an international gallery of shocking murders* Time warner, 2003

French, Yvonne *News from the Past 1805–1887* Gollancz, 1960

Palmer, Roy *A Touch on the Times* Penguin Education, 1974

Pike, E. Royston *Human Documents on the Industrial Revolution* Unwin, 1966

White, R.J. *Waterloo to Peterloo* Peregrine, 1957